Remington Pace

# PyTorch for Deep Learning

## Building Neural Networks and AI Models

First Edition Published in 2026

# TABLE OF CONTENT

# Introduction

# Why PyTorch? Your Roadmap to Deep Learning Mastery

Welcome to the start of your deep learning journey with **PyTorch**. This chapter lays the foundation for everything you'll learn in this book. We'll answer the big questions: *Why deep learning? Why PyTorch?* And most importantly, *how will this book turn you into a job-ready deep learning engineer?*

By the end of this chapter, you'll understand:

- What deep learning is and why it's transforming industries.
- Why PyTorch is the go-to tool for researchers and engineers at Tesla, OpenAI, and Meta.
- Who this book is for and what you'll achieve.
- How to set up your development environment.
- How to use this book effectively with hands-on coding and real projects.

Let's begin.

---

## The Rise of Deep Learning

**Deep learning** is a subset of machine learning that uses **neural networks**—computational models inspired by the human brain—to learn patterns from data. Unlike traditional programming, where you write rules, deep learning lets the model *learn* rules directly from examples.

### A Simple Example: Handwritten Digits

Imagine you want a computer to recognize handwritten digits (0–9).

With traditional programming, you'd write complex rules:

> "If the top-left pixel cluster is dark and the center is hollow, it might be an 8..."

With **deep learning**, you:

1. Feed the model thousands of labeled images.
2. Let it adjust internal weights through training.
3. Get a system that recognizes digits with 99%+ accuracy—without handcrafted rules.

This is the power of deep learning.

### Real-World Impact

- **Tesla**: Uses deep learning for **Autopilot**—object detection, lane tracking, and decision-making in real time.
- **OpenAI**: Built **GPT models** using PyTorch to generate human-like text.
- **Meta AI**: Powers **image recognition** in Instagram, **translation** in WhatsApp, and **augmented reality** filters.

Deep learning isn't just academic—it's deployed in production at scale.

---

# PyTorch: The Industry Standard

**PyTorch** is an open-source deep learning framework developed by Facebook (now Meta) in 2016. It's now the **most popular framework** among researchers and increasingly in production.

## Why PyTorch Wins

| Feature | PyTorch Advantage |
|---|---|
| **Dynamic Computation Graph** | Code runs as you write it—perfect for debugging and experimentation. |
| **Pythonic & Intuitive** | Feels like NumPy + GPU acceleration. |
| **Research → Production** | Used in papers at NeurIPS, then deployed via TorchScript. |
| **Strong Ecosystem** | Hugging Face, PyTorch Lightning, TorchVision, etc. |

> **Fact**: Over **70% of accepted papers** at top AI conferences (NeurIPS, ICML) use PyTorch.

### Case Studies

#### Tesla: Full Self-Driving (FSD)

- Uses PyTorch to train **vision models** on millions of driving clips.
- Real-time inference on custom **Dojo supercomputer**.
- Engineers iterate fast using PyTorch's dynamic graphs.

#### OpenAI: GPT and DALL·E

- Trained **GPT-3** and **DALL·E** using PyTorch.
- Leveraged **distributed training** and **mixed precision**.
- Researchers prototype in days, not weeks.

#### Meta: Seamless AI

- PyTorch powers **FAIR (Fundamental AI Research)**.
- Models like **Detectron2** (object detection) and **PyText** (NLP) are open-sourced.
- Seamless transition from research to Instagram/Facebook products.

---

## Who This Book Is For

This book is designed for **three types of learners**:

### 1. Absolute Beginners

- You know basic Python.
- You've heard of AI but never built a neural network.
- You want **clear, step-by-step guidance**.

### 2. Intermediate Learners

- You've tried TensorFlow or scikit-learn.
- You want to **master PyTorch** and build real projects.
- You aim to **stand out in job applications**.

### 3. Aspiring Deep Learning Engineers

- You want **production-ready skills**.
- You need a **portfolio** of deployed models.
- You're targeting roles at FAANG, startups, or AI labs.

**No PhD required.** Just curiosity and a willingness to code.

---

## What You'll Gain

By the end of this book, you will:

### Technical Skills

- Build neural networks from scratch.
- Train models on CPU and GPU.
- Use **transfer learning** to solve problems with little data.

- Deploy models as web apps and APIs.

### Practical Projects

You'll complete **three milestone projects**:

1. **FoodVision Mini**: Classify 101 food types (computer vision).
2. **Paper Replicator**: Reproduce a research paper model.
3. **FoodVision Pro**: Deploy a production-grade food classifier.

### Career-Ready Portfolio

- GitHub repo with clean, modular code.
- Live demos (Streamlit, Hugging Face).
- Experiment logs (Weights & Biases).
- Resume bullet points that get interviews.

---

# Tools Setup: Your Deep Learning Environment

Let's set up your system. Follow these steps **exactly**.

### Step 1: Install Python (3.9–3.11 recommended)

bash
```
# Check version
python --version
```

Download from python.org if needed.

## Step 2: Create a Virtual Environment

bash

```
python -m venv pytorch-env
source pytorch-env/bin/activate    # Mac/Linux
pytorch-env\Scripts\activate       # Windows
```

## Step 3: Install PyTorch

Go to pytorch.org/get-started

### With GPU (NVIDIA CUDA)

bash

```
pip install torch torchvision torchaudio --index-url
https://download.pytorch.org/whl/cu118
```

### CPU Only

bash

```
pip install torch torchvision torchaudio
```

## Step 4: Install Jupyter and Essentials

bash

```
pip install jupyter matplotlib numpy pandas seaborn scikit-learn
```

## Step 5: Launch Jupyter

bash

```
jupyter notebook
```

Create a new notebook: 01_intro.ipynb

---

## Verify Installation

Run this in a cell:

```python
import torch
x = torch.rand(5, 3)
print(x)
print(torch.cuda.is_available())  # Should print True if GPU is set up
```

**Expected Output**:

```text
tensor([[0.1324, 0.6735, 0.2231],
        [0.8756, 0.4432, 0.1987],
        ...])
True
```

If you see True, your GPU is ready. If False, you're on CPU—still works!

---

# How to Use This Book

This is a **hands-on, code-along book**. Don't just read—**type every line**.

## Learning Workflow

| Step | Action |
|---|---|
| 1 | Read the explanation |
| 2 | Run the provided code |
| 3 | Modify one parameter |
| 4 | Observe the change |

5 Answer the reflection question

## Code Style

- All code is in **Python 3.10+**.
- Uses **Google-style docstrings**.
- Modular, reusable, and production-ready.

## Milestone Projects

| Project | Chapter | Goal |
|---|---|---|
| FoodVision Mini | 4 | 90%+ accuracy on 10 food classes |
| Paper Replication | 9 | Reproduce a CVPR paper |
| FoodVision Pro | 10 | Deploy live web app |

> **Pro Tip**: Push every project to GitHub. Recruiters check repos.

---

# Your First PyTorch Code

Let's write your first neural network input.

```python
import torch
import torch.nn as nn

# Create a tensor (like a NumPy array, but on GPU)
```

```
data = torch.tensor([[1.0, 2.0], [3.0, 4.0]])

# Define a simple linear layer
layer = nn.Linear(in_features=2, out_features=1)

# Forward pass
output = layer(data)
print(output)
```

**Output**:

```
text
tensor([[-0.2341],
      [-0.8765]], grad_fn=<AddmmBackward>)
```

You just ran a **neural network layer**!

---

# Common Mistakes to Avoid

| Mistake | Fix |
|---|---|
| Not activating virtual environment | Always run source pytorch-env/bin/activate |
| Using wrong PyTorch CUDA version | Match your driver (e.g., CUDA 11.8) |
| Forgetting .to(device) | Move model and data to GPU |
| Running on CPU with large data | Use DataLoader with pin_memory=True |
| Not setting random seeds | Use torch.manual_seed(42) |

---

## Summary: Key Takeaways

1. **Deep learning** learns patterns from data using neural networks.
2. **PyTorch** is the leading framework—used by Tesla, OpenAI, and Meta.
3. This book is for **beginners to engineers**—no prior DL knowledge needed.
4. You'll build **3 portfolio projects** and deploy live models.
5. **Set up your environment now**—PyTorch + Jupyter is all you need.
6. **Code along**—don't just read. Type, modify, break, fix.

---

## Practice Exercises

### Exercise 1: Tensor Basics

Create a 3x3 tensor of zeros, then:

- Add 1 to all elements.
- Multiply by 2.
- Move to GPU (if available).
- Print device and shape.

python
```
# Your code here
```

### Exercise 2: Simple Model

Define a linear layer: in=3, out=2
Create random input: batch_size=4

Run forward pass and print output shape.

### Exercise 3: GPU Check

Write a function get_device() that returns 'cuda' if available, else 'cpu'.

---

## Challenge: "Hello, Neural Net!"

Build a model that takes a 1D input (e.g., house size) and predicts price.

python
```
# Pseudocode
input = torch.tensor([[1500.0]]) # sq ft
model = nn.Linear(1, 1)
prediction = model(input)
print(f"Predicted price: ${prediction.item():.2f}")
```

**Goal**: Run it. Then change weights manually to see how output changes.

---

**Next Chapter**: *PyTorch Fundamentals – Building Blocks of Deep Learning*

You'll master **tensors**, **autograd**, and **GPU acceleration**.

Get ready. The journey starts now.

# Chapter 1

# PyTorch Fundamentals – Building Blocks of Deep Learning

Welcome to your first deep dive into **PyTorch**. In this chapter, you'll master **tensors**—the fundamental data structure powering every neural network. Think of tensors as supercharged NumPy arrays with GPU support, automatic differentiation, and seamless integration into deep learning workflows.

By the end of this chapter, you'll be able to:

- Create, manipulate, and operate on tensors with confidence.
- Choose correct data types and avoid memory issues.
- Index and reshape tensors like a pro.
- Run computations on GPU for massive speedups.
- Debug common tensor errors before they crash your model.

Let's begin.

---

# Understanding Tensors: The Core of PyTorch

A **tensor** is a multi-dimensional array. It generalizes:

- **Scalar** → 0D tensor (3.14)
- **Vector** → 1D tensor ([1, 2, 3])
- **Matrix** → 2D tensor ([[1, 2], [3, 4]])
- **Image batch** → 4D tensor ([batch, channels, height, width])

Tensors are the **language of deep learning**.

## Creating Tensors

python
```
import torch

# Scalar
scalar = torch.tensor(42)
print(scalar)          # tensor(42)
print(scalar.ndim)     # 0
print(scalar.shape)    # torch.Size([])

# Vector
vector = torch.tensor([1.0, 2.0, 3.0])
print(vector)          # tensor([1., 2., 3.])
print(vector.shape)    # torch.Size([3])

# Matrix
matrix = torch.tensor([[1, 2],
                       [3, 4]])
print(matrix)
# tensor([[1, 2],
#         [3, 4]])
print(matrix.shape)    # torch.Size([2, 2])

# 3D tensor (e.g., batch of 2 grayscale images, 3x3)
```

```
batch = torch.tensor([[[1, 2, 3],
                       [4, 5, 6],
                       [7, 8, 9]],
                      [[9, 8, 7],
                       [6, 5, 4],
                       [3, 2, 1]]])
print(batch.shape)     # torch.Size([2, 3, 3])
```

> **Real-World Use**: The batch tensor above mimics a batch of two 3x3 grayscale images—common in computer vision.

---

## Tensor Creation Helpers

PyTorch provides shortcuts for common patterns.

```python
# Zeros, ones, and ranges
zeros = torch.zeros(2, 3)
ones = torch.ones(3, 3)
range_tensor = torch.arange(0, 10, step=2)  # [0, 2, 4, 6, 8]

# Random tensors (crucial for weight initialization)
random_normal = torch.randn(3, 3)         # Gaussian
random_uniform = torch.rand(2, 4)         # [0, 1)

# Like another tensor (same shape)
x = torch.randn(2, 3)
x_like = torch.zeros_like(x)
```

> **Pro Tip**: Use torch.randn for model weights. It helps training converge.

---

## PyTorch vs NumPy: A Quick Comparison

| Feature | NumPy | PyTorch |
|---|---|---|
| GPU Support | No | Yes |
| Autograd | No | Yes |
| Deep Learning | No | Yes (nn.Module, etc.) |
| Interoperability | Yes | Yes |

```python
import numpy as np

# NumPy → PyTorch
np_array = np.array([[1, 2], [3, 4]])
tensor_from_np = torch.from_numpy(np_array)

# PyTorch → NumPy
tensor = torch.tensor([[5, 6], [7, 8]])
np_from_tensor = tensor.numpy()
```

> **Warning**: torch.from_numpy() shares memory. Modify one, both change.

---

## PyTorch Data Types

Tensors have **dtypes**. Choosing the right one saves memory and prevents bugs.

```python
# Common dtypes
float32_tensor = torch.tensor([1.0, 2.0], dtype=torch.float32) # Default
```

```
float16_tensor = torch.tensor([1.0, 2.0], dtype=torch.float16) #
Half precision
int64_tensor = torch.tensor([1, 2], dtype=torch.int64)         #
Long
bool_tensor = torch.tensor([True, False], dtype=torch.bool)

print(float32_tensor.dtype) # torch.float32
```

### When to Use Which?

| Use Case | Recommended dtype |
|---|---|
| Model weights, inputs | float32 (default) |
| Large models, memory tight | float16 (mixed precision) |
| Labels, indices | int64 |
| Masks | bool |

> **Actionable Step**: Always check .dtype when loading data.

python
```
x = torch.randn(1000, 1000)
print(f"Memory: {x.element_size() * x.nelement() / 1e6:.2f} MB")
```

---

## Indexing and Slicing

Tensors support NumPy-style indexing.

python
```
x = torch.arange(12).reshape(3, 4)
# tensor([[ 0,  1,  2,  3],
#         [ 4,  5,  6,  7],
#         [ 8,  9, 10, 11]])
```

```python
# Single element
print(x[0, 1])       # tensor(1)

# Row, column
print(x[:, 1])       # tensor([1, 5, 9])
print(x[1, :])       # tensor([4, 5, 6, 7])

# Last row, first two columns
print(x[-1, :2])     # tensor([8, 9])

# Boolean indexing
mask = x > 5
print(x[mask])       # tensor([6, 7, 8, 9, 10, 11])
```

> **Real-World Example**: In image processing, image[:, :, 0] extracts the red channel (if channels last).

---

# Reshaping Tensors

Reshaping changes view without copying data (if contiguous).

```python
x = torch.arange(12)

# Reshape
print(x.reshape(3, 4))
# tensor([[ 0,  1,  2,  3],
#         [ 4,  5,  6,  7],
#         [ 8,  9, 10, 11]])

# View (same as reshape, fails if not contiguous)
print(x.view(4, 3))
```

```python
# Flatten
print(x.flatten())  # or x.view(-1)

# Add dimension
print(x.unsqueeze(0).shape)  # [1, 12]
print(x.unsqueeze(1).shape)  # [12, 1]

# Remove dimension
y = torch.randn(1, 10, 1)
print(y.squeeze().shape)     # [10]
```

**Common Mistake**: Using -1 incorrectly.

python
```python
# Good: Let PyTorch infer
x.reshape(3, -1)  # → [3, 4]

# Bad: Multiple -1
# x.reshape(-1, -1)  # Error!
```

---

# Broadcasting: Automatic Alignment

PyTorch automatically expands dimensions for operations.

python
```python
a = torch.tensor([[1], [2], [3]])   # [3, 1]
b = torch.tensor([10, 20, 30, 40])  # [4]

# a: [3, 1] → [3, 4]
# b: [4]    → [1, 4] → [3, 4]
result = a + b
print(result)
# tensor([[11, 21, 31, 41],
#         [12, 22, 32, 42],
```

```
#       [13, 23, 33, 43]])
```

> **Rule**: Dimensions align from the right.
> Compatible if equal or one is 1.

---

## In-Place Operations

Save memory with in-place methods (_) suffix.

python
```python
x = torch.randn(3, 3)
x.add_(5)      # x = x + 5
x.mul_(2)      # x = x * 2
```

> **Warning**: In-place ops break gradient history.
> Avoid in model definitions.

---

## GPU Acceleration: Leveraging CUDA

Modern GPUs can perform **thousands of operations in parallel**. PyTorch makes GPU usage seamless.

### Check GPU Availability

python
```python
device = torch.device("cuda" if torch.cuda.is_available() else
"cpu")
print(device)  # cuda or cpu
```

## Move Tensors to GPU

```python
x = torch.randn(1000, 1000)

# CPU → GPU
x_gpu = x.to(device)

# Or during creation
x_gpu = torch.randn(1000, 1000, device=device)
```

## Speed Test: CPU vs GPU

```python
import time

def benchmark(tensor):
    start = time.time()
    for _ in range(1000):
        tensor = tensor @ tensor  # Matrix multiply
    torch.cuda.synchronize() if tensor.is_cuda else None
    return time.time() - start

# CPU
cpu_tensor = torch.randn(1000, 1000)
print(f"CPU Time: {benchmark(cpu_tensor):.4f}s")

# GPU
if torch.cuda.is_available():
    gpu_tensor = cpu_tensor.to("cuda")
    print(f"GPU Time: {benchmark(gpu_tensor):.4f}s")
```

**Typical Output**:

```text
CPU Time: 12.4512s
GPU Time: 0.0821s
```

**150x speedup** on matrix operations.

---

### Moving Models and Data Together

python
```
model = nn.Linear(1000, 1000).to(device)
x = torch.randn(64, 1000).to(device)
y = model(x)  # Runs on GPU
```

> **Common Bug**: Forgetting to move **both** model and data.

python
```
# WRONG
model = model.to("cuda")
x = x.to("cpu")  # ← Mismatch!
# y = model(x)   # RuntimeError
```

---

## Hands-On: Simple Tensor Exercises

Open a new Jupyter notebook: 01_tensors.ipynb

### Exercise 1: Create an Image Tensor

python
```
# Simulate a 28x28 grayscale image
image = torch.arange(784).reshape(1, 28, 28).float() / 255.0
print(image.shape)      # [1, 28, 28]
print(image.min(), image.max())
```

### Exercise 2: Batch of RGB Images

python

```
# 4 images, 3 channels, 32x32
batch = torch.rand(4, 3, 32, 32)
print(batch.shape)

# Extract first image, red channel
red_channel = batch[0, 0]  # [32, 32]
```

### Exercise 3: Reshape for Linear Layer

python
```
# Flatten batch for fully connected layer
flattened = batch.view(batch.shape[0], -1)
print(flattened.shape)  # [4, 3072]
```

### Exercise 4: GPU Matrix Multiply

python
```
if torch.cuda.is_available():
    a = torch.randn(500, 500, device="cuda")
    b = torch.randn(500, 500, device="cuda")
    c = a @ b
    print(c.norm())
```

---

# Debugging Common Errors

| Error | Cause | Fix |
|---|---|---|
| RuntimeError: Expected all tensors to be on the same device | Model on GPU, data on CPU | .to(device) for both |
| IndexError: too many indices | Wrong .ndim | Check tensor.shape |

| | | |
|---|---|---|
| RuntimeError: view size is not compatible | Tensor not contiguous | Use .contiguous() before .view() |
| MemoryError | Too large tensor | Use smaller batch, float16, or gradient accumulation |
| NaN in loss | Exploding gradients | Clip gradients, lower learning rate |

### Debug Tip: Print Shapes

python
```python
print(f"Input: {x.shape}, Weight: {model.weight.shape}")
```

---

# Real-World Applications

| Task | Tensor Shape | Example |
|---|---|---|
| Image Classification | [batch, 3, 224, 224] | ResNet input |
| Text Embedding | [batch, seq_len, embed_dim] | BERT |
| Time Series | [batch, timesteps, features] | LSTM |
| 3D Medical Scan | [batch, depth, height, width] | U-Net |

**Actionable Step**: When loading data, always verify:

python
```
print(data.shape, labels.shape, data.dtype)
```

---

## Key Takeaway: Mastering the Core Data Structures

Tensors are the **DNA of deep learning**. Every weight, activation, and gradient is a tensor. Mastering them means:

- Writing efficient, bug-free code.
- Scaling models from laptop to cloud.
- Debugging 90% of errors before training starts.

You now have the tools to:

1. **Create** any tensor shape.
2. **Manipulate** with indexing, reshaping, and broadcasting.
3. **Accelerate** with GPU.
4. **Debug** like a pro.

---

## Summary: Key Takeaways

1. **Tensors** are multi-dimensional arrays with GPU support.
2. Use torch.tensor(), randn, zeros, arange for creation.
3. **Data types matter**: float32 default, float16 for memory, int64 for labels.
4. **Indexing** works like NumPy: tensor[row, col], slicing, boolean masks.

5. **Reshape** with .view(), .reshape(), .flatten(), .unsqueeze().
6. **Broadcasting** auto-expands compatible shapes.
7. **GPU** = 100x+ speed. Always .to(device) model **and** data.
8. **In-place ops** (_) save memory but break gradients.
9. **Debug early**: Print shapes, dtypes, and device.

---

# Practice Exercises

## Exercise 1: Tensor Creator Function

python
```
def create_image_batch(batch_size, height, width,
channels=3):
    """
    Returns a batch of random RGB images.
    Shape: [batch_size, channels, height, width]
    """
    # Your code here
    pass

# Test
batch = create_image_batch(8, 64, 64)
print(batch.shape)  # Should be [8, 3, 64, 64]
```

## Exercise 2: Normalize Batch

python
```
# Given batch in [0, 255], normalize to [0, 1]
pixel_values = torch.randint(0, 256, (4, 3, 32, 32)).float()
normalized = # Your code
print(normalized.min(), normalized.max())  # 0.0, 1.0
```

### Exercise 3: Channel Swap

python
```
# Convert [B, C, H, W] → [B, H, W, C] (for matplotlib)
def to_numpy_image(tensor):
    return tensor.permute(0, 2, 3, 1).numpy()

# Test with one image
img = batch[0]
print(to_numpy_image(img.unsqueeze(0)).shape)
```

---

## Challenge: "Tensor Transformer"

Write a function that:

1. Takes a [3, 224, 224] image tensor.
2. Normalizes pixel values (using ImageNet stats).
3. Adds batch dimension.
4. Moves to GPU if available.
5. Returns the processed tensor.

python
```
def preprocess_image(img_tensor):
    """
    img_tensor: [3, 224, 224], values in [0, 255]
    Returns: [1, 3, 224, 224] on correct device, normalized
    """
    # ImageNet mean/std
    mean = torch.tensor([0.485, 0.456, 0.406])
    std = torch.tensor([0.229, 0.224, 0.225])

    # Your code here
    pass
```

**Test**:

python

```
img = torch.randint(0, 256, (3, 224, 224)).float()
out = preprocess_image(img)
print(out.shape, out.device, out.mean(), out.std())
```

---

**Next Chapter**: *The PyTorch Workflow – From Data to Trained Model*

You'll build your **first trainable model** using everything you learned here.

Keep coding. The neural networks are waiting.

# Chapter 2

# The PyTorch Workflow – From Data to Trained Model

In this chapter, you'll learn the **complete end-to-end PyTorch workflow**—the exact process used by engineers at Tesla, OpenAI, and Meta to go from raw data to a trained, evaluated model.

You'll build your **first trainable model** from scratch using **linear regression** to predict house prices. This is the foundation of every deep learning project—whether you're classifying images, generating text, or forecasting sales.

By the end of this chapter, you'll be able to:

- Follow a **7-step deep learning framework**.
- Load, clean, and preprocess real-world data.
- Build, train, and evaluate a PyTorch model.
- Visualize training progress.
- Integrate PyTorch with **NumPy** and **Pandas**.

Let's get started.

---

# Step-by-Step Problem-Solving Framework

Every deep learning project follows this **7-step cycle**:

```text
1. Problem Definition → 2. Data → 3. Model → 4. Loss & Optimizer
5. Training Loop → 6. Evaluation → 7. Improve/Deploy
```

We'll walk through each step with code.

---

## Step 1: Problem Definition

**Goal**: Predict house price (in thousands) from size (sq ft).

- **Input**: size (1 feature)
- **Output**: price (1 value)
- **Type**: **Regression**

```python
# Example data
size = [750, 900, 1200, 1500, 2000]   # sq ft
price = [110, 130, 180, 220, 300]     # $1000s
```

---

## Step 2: Get Data

We'll use synthetic data first, then real-world data.

```python
import torch
import numpy as np
import matplotlib.pyplot as plt
```

```
# Set random seed for reproducibility
torch.manual_seed(42)

# Generate synthetic data
X = torch.arange(700, 2500, 100).float().unsqueeze(1)  # [N, 1]
weight = 0.15
bias = 50
y = weight * X + bias + torch.randn_like(X) * 20      # Add noise
```

---

# Data Preparation: Loading, Splitting, and Preprocessing

Real data is messy. We must **clean**, **split**, and **convert**.

## 2.1: Train/Val/Test Split

python

```
from sklearn.model_selection import train_test_split

# Convert to NumPy first
X_np, y_np = X.numpy(), y.numpy()

# 80% train, 10% val, 10% test
X_train, X_temp, y_train, y_temp = train_test_split(
   X_np, y_np, test_size=0.2, random_state=42)
X_val, X_test, y_val, y_test = train_test_split(
   X_temp, y_temp, test_size=0.5, random_state=42)

# Back to PyTorch
X_train = torch.from_numpy(X_train)
y_train = torch.from_numpy(y_train)
X_val = torch.from_numpy(X_val)
y_val = torch.from_numpy(y_val)
X_test = torch.from_numpy(X_test)
y_test = torch.from_numpy(y_test)
```

**Why split?** Prevent **data leakage**—model must generalize.

---

## 2.2: Create Dataset and DataLoader

python
```
from torch.utils.data import TensorDataset, DataLoader

# Combine features and labels
train_ds = TensorDataset(X_train, y_train)
val_ds = TensorDataset(X_val, y_val)
test_ds = TensorDataset(X_test, y_test)

# Batch data
BATCH_SIZE = 8
train_loader = DataLoader(train_ds, batch_size=BATCH_SIZE,
shuffle=True)
val_loader = DataLoader(val_ds, batch_size=BATCH_SIZE)
test_loader = DataLoader(test_ds, batch_size=BATCH_SIZE)
```

**Actionable Step**: Always **shuffle training data**, never validation/test.

---

## 2.3: Preprocessing (Normalization)

Models train faster with **zero mean, unit variance**.

python
```
def normalize(tensor):
    mean = tensor.mean()
    std = tensor.std()
    return (tensor - mean) / std

X_train_norm = normalize(X_train)
X_val_norm = normalize(X_val)
```

X_test_norm = normalize(X_test)

> **Warning**: Fit normalization on **train only**, apply to val/test.

---

## Building Your First Model: Linear Regression

python
```
import torch.nn as nn

class LinearRegression(nn.Module):
    def __init__(self):
        super().__init__()
        self.linear = nn.Linear(in_features=1, out_features=1)

    def forward(self, x):
        return self.linear(x)

# Instantiate
model = LinearRegression()
print(model)
# LinearRegression(
#   (linear): Linear(in_features=1, out_features=1, bias=True)
# )
```

### Model Parameters

python
```
print(f"Weight: {model.linear.weight.item():.4f}")
print(f"Bias: {model.linear.bias.item():.4f}")
```

---

# Loss Function and Optimizer

## Loss: Mean Squared Error (MSE)

python
```
loss_fn = nn.MSELoss()
```

## Optimizer: Stochastic Gradient Descent (SGD)

python
```
optimizer = torch.optim.SGD(model.parameters(), lr=0.01)
```

> **Learning rate tip**: Start with 0.01. Too high → diverges. Too low → slow.

---

# Training Loop

python
```
# Device
device = "cuda" if torch.cuda.is_available() else "cpu"
model.to(device)

# Training mode
model.train()

# Epochs
EPOCHS = 100

for epoch in range(EPOCHS):
    epoch_loss = 0
    for X_batch, y_batch in train_loader:
        X_batch, y_batch = X_batch.to(device), y_batch.to(device)

        # 1. Forward pass
        y_pred = model(X_batch)
```

```
        # 2. Loss
        loss = loss_fn(y_pred, y_batch)

        # 3. Zero gradients
        optimizer.zero_grad()

        # 4. Backward pass
        loss.backward()

        # 5. Update weights
        optimizer.step()

        epoch_loss += loss.item()

    if epoch % 20 == 0:
        print(f"Epoch {epoch} | Train Loss:
{epoch_loss/len(train_loader):.4f}")
```

---

# Evaluation Loop

```python
model.eval()  # Disable dropout, batchnorm updates
val_loss = 0

with torch.inference_mode():  # No gradients
    for X_val_b, y_val_b in val_loader:
        X_val_b, y_val_b = X_val_b.to(device), y_val_b.to(device)
        y_pred = model(X_val_b)
        val_loss += loss_fn(y_pred, y_val_b).item()

print(f"Validation Loss: {val_loss/len(val_loader):.4f}")
```

> **Use torch.inference_mode()** in evaluation—faster, less memory.

---

# Evaluation Metrics

## 1. Mean Absolute Error (MAE)

```python
mae = nn.L1Loss()
# Measures average $|error|$ in same units as target
```

## 2. R² Score (Coefficient of Determination)

```python
from torchmetrics import R2Score

r2 = R2Score()
# 1.0 = perfect, 0.0 = mean baseline
```

## 3. Visualization

```python
model.eval()
with torch.inference_mode():
    y_pred = model(X_test.to(device)).cpu()

plt.scatter(X_test, y_test, c="blue", label="True")
plt.scatter(X_test, y_pred, c="red", label="Pred")
plt.plot(X_test, y_test, "b-", alpha=0.3)
plt.xlabel("Size (sq ft)")
plt.ylabel("Price ($1000)")
plt.legend()
plt.show()
```

---

# Hands-On Project: Predicting House Prices with a Basic Model

Let's build a **complete, reusable script**.

## house_price_model.py

python
```
# house_price_model.py
import torch
import torch.nn as nn
from torch.utils.data import DataLoader, TensorDataset
import numpy as np
import matplotlib.pyplot as plt

# 1. Data
X = torch.arange(700, 2500, 50).float().unsqueeze(1)
y = 0.15 * X + 50 + torch.randn_like(X) * 25

# 2. Split
from sklearn.model_selection import train_test_split
X_train, X_temp, y_train, y_temp = train_test_split(X, y,
test_size=0.3, random_state=42)
X_val, X_test, y_val, y_test = train_test_split(X_temp, y_temp,
test_size=0.5, random_state=42)

# 3. Normalize
def normalize_train_val(train, val, test):
  mean = train.mean()
  std = train.std()
  return (train - mean)/std, (val - mean)/std, (test - mean)/std

X_train_n, X_val_n, X_test_n = normalize_train_val(X_train,
X_val, X_test)

# 4. Datasets
train_ds = TensorDataset(X_train_n, y_train)
val_ds = TensorDataset(X_val_n, y_val)
```

```
test_ds = TensorDataset(X_test_n, y_test)

train_loader = DataLoader(train_ds, batch_size=8,
shuffle=True)
val_loader = DataLoader(val_ds, batch_size=8)
test_loader = DataLoader(test_ds, batch_size=8)

# 5. Model
class HousePricePredictor(nn.Module):
    def __init__(self):
        super().__init__()
        self.linear = nn.Linear(1, 1)

    def forward(self, x):
        return self.linear(x)

model = HousePricePredictor()
device = "cuda" if torch.cuda.is_available() else "cpu"
model.to(device)

# 6. Loss & Optimizer
loss_fn = nn.MSELoss()
optimizer = torch.optim.SGD(model.parameters(), lr=0.01)

# 7. Training
EPOCHS = 200
train_losses = []
val_losses = []

for epoch in range(EPOCHS):
    # Train
    model.train()
    train_loss = 0
    for X_b, y_b in train_loader:
        X_b, y_b = X_b.to(device), y_b.to(device)
        pred = model(X_b)
        loss = loss_fn(pred, y_b)
        optimizer.zero_grad()
        loss.backward()
        optimizer.step()
```

```
        train_loss += loss.item()
    train_loss /= len(train_loader)
    train_losses.append(train_loss)

    # Val
    model.eval()
    val_loss = 0
    with torch.inference_mode():
        for X_b, y_b in val_loader:
            X_b, y_b = X_b.to(device), y_b.to(device)
            pred = model(X_b)
            val_loss += loss_fn(pred, y_b).item()
    val_loss /= len(val_loader)
    val_losses.append(val_loss)

    if epoch % 50 == 0:
        print(f"Epoch {epoch} | Train Loss: {train_loss:.4f} | Val
Loss: {val_loss:.4f}")

# 8. Plot
plt.plot(train_losses, label="Train Loss")
plt.plot(val_losses, label="Val Loss")
plt.xlabel("Epoch")
plt.ylabel("MSE Loss")
plt.legend()
plt.show()

# 9. Final Test
model.eval()
with torch.inference_mode():
    test_pred = model(X_test_n.to(device)).cpu()
    test_mae = nn.L1Loss()(test_pred, y_test)
    print(f"Test MAE: ${test_mae.item()*1000:.2f}")
```

**Run**:

bash
```
python house_price_model.py
```

---

# Advanced Tip: Integrating PyTorch with NumPy and Pandas

Real data lives in **CSV files**. Use **Pandas**.

## Load Real House Data

```python
import pandas as pd

# Download sample:
https://raw.githubusercontent.com/mrdbourke/pytorch-deep-learning/main/data/house_prices.csv
df = pd.read_csv("house_prices.csv")

# Select features
features = ["GrLivArea", "YearBuilt", "BedroomAbvGr"]
X = df[features].values
y = df["SalePrice"].values / 1000  # in $1000s

# To PyTorch
X_tensor = torch.from_numpy(X).float()
y_tensor = torch.from_numpy(y).float().unsqueeze(1)
```

> **Actionable Step**: Always check for **missing values**:
>
> ```python
> df.isna().sum()
> ```

---

## Common Mistakes to Avoid

| Mistake | Fix |
|---|---|
| **Forgetting .to(device)** | Move **model and data** |
| **Evaluating in train mode** | Use model.eval() + inference_mode() |
| **Data leakage** | Normalize using **train stats only** |
| **Not shuffling** | shuffle=True in train loader |
| **Overfitting** | Monitor val loss, use early stopping |
| **Wrong loss** | Use MSELoss for regression, CrossEntropyLoss for classification |

---

## Real-World Applications

| Task | Input | Output | Loss |
|---|---|---|---|
| House Price | Size, rooms | Price | MSE |
| Stock Prediction | Past prices | Future price | MSE |
| Medical Cost | Age, BMI | Cost | MSE |
| Image Brightness | Image | Scalar | MSE |

---

## Summary: Key Takeaways

1. **7-Step Workflow**: Problem → Data → Model → Loss → Train → Eval → Improve.
2. **Split data** into train/val/test → prevents overfitting.
3. **Normalize** using **train stats only**.
4. **DataLoader** handles batching and shuffling.
5. **Model**: nn.Module with forward().
6. **Loss + Optimizer** → MSELoss, SGD.
7. **Training Loop**: forward → loss → backward → step.
8. **Evaluation**: model.eval() + torch.inference_mode().
9. **Visualize** loss curves and predictions.
10. **Pandas** → **PyTorch** for real data.

---

## Practice Exercises

### Exercise 1: Modify Learning Rate

Change lr=0.1, 0.001, 0.0001. Plot loss curves. Which converges fastest?

### Exercise 2: Add Bias Term Manually

Replace nn.Linear with:

python
```
self.weight = nn.Parameter(torch.randn(1))
self.bias = nn.Parameter(torch.randn(1))
```

Implement forward pass. Compare results.

### Exercise 3: Early Stopping

Stop training if val loss doesn't improve for 10 epochs.

```python
best_loss = float('inf')
patience = 10
wait = 0
```

---

## Challenge: "Multi-Feature House Predictor"

1. Use **3 features**: GrLivArea, BedroomAbvGr, YearBuilt.
2. Normalize each feature.
3. Train model.
4. Compute **MAE in dollars**.
5. Plot true vs predicted prices.

```python
# Load data
df = pd.read_csv("house_prices.csv")
# Your code here
```

**Goal**: MAE < $30,000

---

**Next Chapter**: *Neural Network Classification – Predicting Categories*

You'll classify **handwritten digits** and **clothing items** using real datasets.

Keep training. Your model is learning.

# Chapter 3

# Neural Network Classification – Predicting Categories with PyTorch

In this chapter, you'll build your **first classification neural network** using **Multi-Layer Perceptrons (MLPs)**. You'll go from raw image data to a model that predicts clothing categories with over **85% accuracy** on the **Fashion MNIST** dataset.

This is the foundation of **computer vision**, **spam detection**, **medical diagnosis**, and **sentiment analysis**.

By the end of this chapter, you'll be able to:

- Build an MLP from scratch with nn.Module.
- Use **activation functions** to add non-linearity.
- Understand **backpropagation** and **optimizers**.
- Train **binary** and **multi-class** classifiers.
- Handle **imbalanced data** and **overfitting**.
- Evaluate with **accuracy**, **confusion matrix**, and **precision/recall**.

Let's classify.

---

# From Scratch: Constructing Multi-Layer Perceptrons (MLPs)

An **MLP** is a stack of **fully connected layers** (also called **dense layers**). Each neuron connects to every neuron in the next layer.

## Structure

text

```
Input Layer (784) → Hidden Layer 1 (128) → ReLU → Hidden Layer 2 (64) → ReLU → Output Layer (10)
```

- **Input**: Flattened 28×28 image → 784 features
- **Hidden layers**: Learn patterns
- **Output**: 10 logits (one per class)

---

## Build the MLP

python

```python
import torch
import torch.nn as nn

class FashionClassifier(nn.Module):
    def __init__(self, input_features=784, hidden1=128,
hidden2=64, output_features=10):
        super().__init__()
        self.layer_stack = nn.Sequential(
            nn.Linear(input_features, hidden1),
            nn.ReLU(),
            nn.Linear(hidden1, hidden2),
            nn.ReLU(),
            nn.Linear(hidden2, output_features)
        )

    def forward(self, x):
```

```python
return self.layer_stack(x) # Returns logits
```

**Actionable Step**: Always use nn.Sequential for simple feed-forward models.

---

## Activation Functions: Adding Non-Linearity

Without activation functions, stacking linear layers = one big linear layer → **no learning power**.

### ReLU (Rectified Linear Unit)

python
```python
nn.ReLU() # max(0, x)
```

- **Simple**, **fast**, **prevents vanishing gradients**.
- **Dead neurons** if input always < 0 → use **LeakyReLU** sometimes.

### Others

| Function | Code | Use Case |
|---|---|---|
| Sigmoid | nn.Sigmoid() | Binary output (0–1) |
| Softmax | nn.Softmax(dim=1) | Convert logits → probabilities |
| Tanh | nn.Tanh() | Hidden layers (rare) |

**Never use Softmax in loss** if using CrossEntropyLoss — it includes it.

---

# Backpropagation and Optimizers

## How Learning Happens

1. **Forward pass**: Compute prediction.
2. **Loss**: Compare to true label.
3. **Backward pass**: Compute gradients (loss.backward()).
4. **Update weights**: optimizer.step().

## Optimizers

```python
optimizer = torch.optim.SGD(model.parameters(), lr=0.1)
# or
optimizer = torch.optim.Adam(model.parameters(), lr=0.001)
```

| Optimizer | When to Use |
|---|---|
| **SGD** | Simple, stable |
| **Adam** | Faster, default choice |

**Start with Adam, lr=0.001**

---

# Binary vs Multi-Class Classification

| Type | Output | Loss Function | Example |
|---|---|---|---|

| **Binary** | 1 neuron + Sigmoid | BCEWithLogitsLoss | Spam/Not Spam |
|---|---|---|---|
| **Multi-Class** | N neurons + Softmax | CrossEntropyLoss | 10 clothing types |

---

# Fashion MNIST: Real Dataset Walkthrough

## Load and Explore

python
```
from torchvision import datasets, transforms
from torch.utils.data import DataLoader
import matplotlib.pyplot as plt

# Transform: ToTensor + Normalize
transform = transforms.Compose([
    transforms.ToTensor(),
    transforms.Normalize((0.2859,), (0.3530,))  # Fashion MNIST
stats
])

# Download
train_data = datasets.FashionMNIST(root="data", train=True,
download=True, transform=transform)
test_data = datasets.FashionMNIST(root="data", train=False,
download=True, transform=transform)

# DataLoaders
BATCH_SIZE = 32
train_loader = DataLoader(train_data,
batch_size=BATCH_SIZE, shuffle=True)
test_loader = DataLoader(test_data, batch_size=BATCH_SIZE,
shuffle=False)
```

```
# Visualize
images, labels = next(iter(train_loader))
plt.figure(figsize=(10, 10))
for i in range(16):
    plt.subplot(4, 4, i+1)
    plt.imshow(images[i].squeeze(), cmap="gray")
    plt.title(f"Label: {labels[i].item()}")
    plt.axis("off")
plt.show()
```

**Classes**: T-shirt, Trouser, Pullover, Dress, Coat, Sandal, Shirt, Sneaker, Bag, Ankle boot

---

# Training Loop for Classification

python

```
# Device
device = "cuda" if torch.cuda.is_available() else "cpu"

# Model, loss, optimizer
model = FashionClassifier().to(device)
loss_fn = nn.CrossEntropyLoss()
optimizer = torch.optim.Adam(model.parameters(), lr=0.001)

# Training
EPOCHS = 10
for epoch in range(EPOCHS):
    model.train()
    train_loss, train_acc = 0, 0
    for X, y in train_loader:
        X, y = X.to(device), y.to(device)

        # Flatten image: [B, 1, 28, 28] → [B, 784]
        X = X.view(X.size(0), -1)

        # Forward
        logits = model(X)
```

```
        loss = loss_fn(logits, y)

        # Backward
        optimizer.zero_grad()
        loss.backward()
        optimizer.step()

        train_loss += loss.item()
        train_acc += (logits.argmax(dim=1) == y).sum().item()

    train_loss /= len(train_loader)
    train_acc /= len(train_loader.dataset)

    # Validation
    model.eval()
    val_loss, val_acc = 0, 0
    with torch.inference_mode():
        for X, y in test_loader:
            X, y = X.to(device), y.to(device)
            X = X.view(X.size(0), -1)
            logits = model(X)
            loss = loss_fn(logits, y)
            val_loss += loss.item()
            val_acc += (logits.argmax(dim=1) == y).sum().item()

    val_loss /= len(test_loader)
    val_acc /= len(test_loader.dataset)

    print(f"Epoch {epoch+1} | Train Loss: {train_loss:.4f}, Acc:
{train_acc:.4f} | Val Loss: {val_loss:.4f}, Acc: {val_acc:.4f}")
```

**Expected Output**:

```text
Epoch 10 | Train Acc: 0.8921 | Val Acc: 0.8750
```

---

# Evaluation Metrics

## 1. Accuracy

python
```
def accuracy_fn(y_true, y_pred):
    return (y_true == y_pred).float().mean().item()
```

## 2. Confusion Matrix

python
```
from sklearn.metrics import confusion_matrix
import seaborn as sns

model.eval()
all_preds, all_labels = [], []
with torch.inference_mode():
    for X, y in test_loader:
        X = X.view(X.size(0), -1).to(device)
        logits = model(X)
        preds = logits.argmax(dim=1).cpu()
        all_preds.extend(preds)
        all_labels.extend(y)

cm = confusion_matrix(all_labels, all_preds)
plt.figure(figsize=(10, 8))
sns.heatmap(cm, annot=True, fmt="d", cmap="Blues")
plt.xlabel("Predicted")
plt.ylabel("True")
plt.show()
```

> **Insight**: Shirts often confused with T-shirts.

---

## 3. Precision, Recall, F1

python
```
from sklearn.metrics import classification_report
```

```python
print(classification_report(all_labels, all_preds,
target_names=train_data.classes))
```

---

# Handling Imbalanced Data

## Problem

Suppose 90% of emails are **not spam**. A dumb model predicts “not spam” always → 90% accuracy, but useless.

## Solutions

### 1. Class Weights

python
```python
class_counts = torch.bincount(torch.tensor(train_data.targets))
class_weights = 1. / class_counts.float()
weights = class_weights[torch.tensor(train_data.targets)]

from torch.utils.data import WeightedRandomSampler
sampler = WeightedRandomSampler(weights, len(weights))
train_loader = DataLoader(train_data, batch_size=32,
sampler=sampler)
```

### 2. Oversampling / Undersampling

Use torch.utils.data.Subset or imblearn.

---

# Overfitting Prevention

## Symptoms

- Train acc: 95%, Val acc: 78%

## Fixes

### 1. Early Stopping

python
```
best_val_loss = float('inf')
patience = 3
wait = 0

for epoch in range(EPOCHS):
    # ... training ...
    if val_loss < best_val_loss:
        best_val_loss = val_loss
        wait = 0
        torch.save(model.state_dict(), "best_model.pth")
    else:
        wait += 1
        if wait >= patience:
            print("Early stopping!")
            break
```

### 2. Dropout

python
```
nn.Dropout(p=0.5)  # Randomly zeros 50% of neurons
```

Add after ReLU:

python
```
nn.Sequential(
    nn.Linear(784, 128),
    nn.ReLU(),
    nn.Dropout(0.3),
    ...
)
```

### 3. Weight Decay (L2 Regularization)

python

```
optimizer = torch.optim.Adam(model.parameters(), lr=0.001,
weight_decay=1e-5)
```

---

# Hands-On: Classifying Images of Clothing Items End-to-End

## Full Script: fashion_mnist_classifier.py

python

```
# fashion_mnist_classifier.py
import torch
import torch.nn as nn
from torchvision import datasets, transforms
from torch.utils.data import DataLoader
import matplotlib.pyplot as plt
from sklearn.metrics import confusion_matrix
import seaborn as sns
import numpy as np

# 1. Data
transform = transforms.Compose([
    transforms.ToTensor(),
    transforms.Normalize((0.2859,), (0.3530,))
])

train_data = datasets.FashionMNIST(root="data", train=True,
download=True, transform=transform)
test_data = datasets.FashionMNIST(root="data", train=False,
download=True, transform=transform)

train_loader = DataLoader(train_data, batch_size=64,
shuffle=True)
test_loader = DataLoader(test_data, batch_size=64,
shuffle=False)

# 2. Model
```

```
class FashionMLP(nn.Module):
    def __init__(self):
        super().__init__()
        self.net = nn.Sequential(
            nn.Flatten(),
            nn.Linear(784, 256),
            nn.ReLU(),
            nn.Dropout(0.3),
            nn.Linear(256, 128),
            nn.ReLU(),
            nn.Dropout(0.3),
            nn.Linear(128, 10)
        )

    def forward(self, x):
        return self.net(x)

model = FashionMLP()
device = "cuda" if torch.cuda.is_available() else "cpu"
model.to(device)

# 3. Loss & Optimizer
loss_fn = nn.CrossEntropyLoss()
optimizer = torch.optim.Adam(model.parameters(), lr=0.001,
weight_decay=1e-5)

# 4. Training
EPOCHS = 20
best_val_acc = 0
for epoch in range(EPOCHS):
    model.train()
    for X, y in train_loader:
        X, y = X.to(device), y.to(device)
        logits = model(X)
        loss = loss_fn(logits, y)
        optimizer.zero_grad()
        loss.backward()
        optimizer.step()

    # Eval
```

```
    model.eval()
    correct = 0
    with torch.inference_mode():
        for X, y in test_loader:
            X, y = X.to(device), y.to(device)
            logits = model(X)
            pred = logits.argmax(dim=1)
            correct += (pred == y).sum().item()
    acc = correct / len(test_loader.dataset)

    if acc > best_val_acc:
        best_val_acc = acc
        torch.save(model.state_dict(), "best_fashion_model.pth")

    print(f"Epoch {epoch+1} | Test Acc: {acc:.4f}")

print(f"Best Accuracy: {best_val_acc:.4f}")
```

**Run**:

bash
```
python fashion_mnist_classifier.py
```

---

## Pro Insight: Classification vs Regression

| Task | Output | Loss | Example |
|---|---|---|---|
| **Classification** | Category | CrossEntropy, BCE | "Cat or Dog?" |
| **Regression** | Number | MSE, MAE | "House price?" |

### When to Use Which?

| Question | Answer Type | Use |
|---|---|---|
| "Is this email spam?" | Yes/No | Binary Classification |
| "What digit is this?" | 0–9 | Multi-Class |
| "How much will this house sell for?" | $350,000 | Regression |
| "How likely is click?" | 0.0–1.0 | Regression or Binary (threshold) |

> **Tip**: If output is **bounded** (0–1), consider **regression + sigmoid**.

---

# Common Mistakes to Avoid

| Mistake | Fix |
|---|---|
| **Forgetting Flatten()** | Images are 4D → must flatten |
| **Using Softmax + CrossEntropyLoss** | CrossEntropyLoss expects **logits** |
| **Not normalizing data** | Fashion MNIST needs (0.2859, 0.3530) |
| **Evaluating in train mode** | model.eval() + inference_mode() |
| **Class imbalance ignored** | Use weights or sampling |

| **No early stopping** | Save best model |
|---|---|

## Real-World Applications

| App | Input | Classes | Model |
|---|---|---|---|
| Medical Diagnosis | X-ray | Pneumonia / Normal | Binary CNN |
| Sentiment Analysis | Review text | Positive / Negative / Neutral | Transformer |
| Fraud Detection | Transaction | Fraud / Legit | MLP |
| Object Detection | Image | 80 COCO classes | YOLO |

## Summary: Key Takeaways

1. **MLP** = stack of Linear → ReLU → Linear.
2. **Activation functions** (ReLU) add non-linearity.
3. **Backpropagation** computes gradients → optimizer updates.
4. **Binary**: 1 output + BCE. **Multi-class**: N outputs + CrossEntropy.
5. **Fashion MNIST** = real image classification benchmark.
6. **DataLoader** + shuffle=True for training.
7. **Evaluation**: accuracy, confusion matrix, precision/recall.
8. **Overfitting fixes**: Dropout, weight decay, early stopping.

9. **Imbalanced data**: class weights or sampling.
10. **Classification** for categories, **regression** for numbers.

---

# Practice Exercises

## Exercise 1: Binary Classifier

Convert Fashion MNIST to **binary**: T-shirt (1) vs Trouser (0).

python
```
# Filter data
binary_train = [(x, 1 if y == 0 else 0) for x, y in train_data if y in [0, 1]]
# Use BCEWithLogitsLoss, 1 output neuron
```

## Exercise 2: Add BatchNorm

python
```
nn.BatchNorm1d(128)  # After Linear, before ReLU
```

Does it help convergence?

## Exercise 3: Learning Rate Scheduler

python
```
scheduler = torch.optim.lr_scheduler.StepLR(optimizer, step_size=5, gamma=0.5)
scheduler.step()  # After epoch
```

---

## Challenge: "Shirt vs T-Shirt Binary Classifier"

1. Filter only **Shirt (6)** and **T-shirt (0)**.
2. Build binary MLP.
3. Use **class weights**.
4. Achieve **>95% accuracy**.
5. Plot **ROC curve**.

python
```python
from sklearn.metrics import roc_curve, auc
# Your code
```

---

**Next Chapter**: *PyTorch for Computer Vision – CNNs and Transfer Learning*

You'll crush **FoodVision** with **95%+ accuracy**.

Your classifier is ready. Deploy it.

# Chapter 4

# PyTorch for Computer Vision – Seeing the World Through Neural Nets

In this chapter, you'll master **Convolutional Neural Networks (CNNs)**—the backbone of modern **image classification**, **object detection**, **medical imaging**, and **autonomous driving**.

You'll build **FoodVision Mini**: a custom image classifier that identifies **10 types of food** (Pizza, Steak, Sushi, etc.) with **>85% accuracy** using real-world images.

By the end of this chapter, you'll be able to:

- Understand how **convolutions** extract visual features.
- Build **CNNs** from scratch with nn.Conv2d, pooling, and fully connected layers.
- Use **data augmentation** to make models robust.
- Apply **transfer learning** to boost performance with little data.
- Evaluate models with **confusion matrices**, **precision/recall**, and **visualizations**.
- Deploy a **food classifier** end-to-end.

Let's see like a neural network.

---

# Convolutional Neural Networks (CNNs): How Machines "See"

Traditional MLPs (from Chapter 3) treat images as flat vectors → **lose spatial structure**.

**CNNs** preserve 2D structure using **convolutions**.

## What Is a Convolution?

A **filter** (small matrix, e.g., 3×3) slides over the image, computing **dot products** to detect patterns.

python
```
import torch
import torch.nn.functional as F

# Sample 1-channel image (grayscale)
image = torch.rand(1, 1, 28, 28)  # [batch, channels, H, W]

# 3x3 edge detection filter
kernel = torch.tensor([[[[-1, -1, -1],
                    [ -1,  8, -1],
                    [ -1, -1, -1]]]], dtype=torch.float32)

# Apply convolution
feature_map = F.conv2d(image, kernel, padding=1)
print(feature_map.shape)  # [1, 1, 28, 28]
```

> **Real-World**: This filter detects **edges**. Others detect corners, textures, etc.

---

## CNN Building Blocks

| Layer | Purpose | Code |
| --- | --- | --- |
| nn.Conv2d | Learn spatial features | in_channels, out_channels, kernel_size |
| nn.ReLU | Non-linearity | |
| nn.MaxPool2d | Downsample, reduce computation | kernel_size=2 |
| nn.Flatten | Prepare for fully connected layer | |
| nn.Linear | Classification head | |

---

## A Simple CNN Architecture

python
```
import torch.nn as nn

class TinyCNN(nn.Module):
  def __init__(self, input_channels=3, num_classes=10):
    super().__init__()
    self.conv_block1 = nn.Sequential(
      nn.Conv2d(input_channels, 32, kernel_size=3,
padding=1),
      nn.ReLU(),
      nn.Conv2d(32, 64, kernel_size=3, padding=1),
      nn.ReLU(),
      nn.MaxPool2d(2)  # 224 → 112
    )
    self.conv_block2 = nn.Sequential(
      nn.Conv2d(64, 128, kernel_size=3, padding=1),
```

```
            nn.ReLU(),
            nn.MaxPool2d(2)  # 112 → 56
        )
        self.classifier = nn.Sequential(
            nn.Flatten(),
            nn.Linear(128 * 56 * 56, 512),
            nn.ReLU(),
            nn.Linear(512, num_classes)
        )

    def forward(self, x):
        x = self.conv_block1(x)
        x = self.conv_block2(x)
        x = self.classifier(x)
        return x
```

**Note**: Final linear layer size depends on **input image size** after pooling.

---

# Data Augmentation: Making Models Robust

Real-world images vary in lighting, angle, crop. **Augmentation** simulates this during training.

## Common Augmentations

| Transform | Purpose |
|---|---|
| RandomResizedCrop | Zoom + crop |
| RandomHorizontalFlip | Mirror images |
| ColorJitter | Change brightness, contrast |

| RandomRotation | Rotate slightly |
|---|---|

python
```python
from torchvision import transforms

train_transform = transforms.Compose([
    transforms.Resize(256),
    transforms.RandomResizedCrop(224),
    transforms.RandomHorizontalFlip(p=0.5),
    transforms.ColorJitter(brightness=0.2, contrast=0.2),
    transforms.ToTensor(),
    transforms.Normalize(mean=[0.485, 0.456, 0.406],
                std=[0.229, 0.224, 0.225])
])

test_transform = transforms.Compose([
    transforms.Resize(256),
    transforms.CenterCrop(224),
    transforms.ToTensor(),
    transforms.Normalize(mean=[0.485, 0.456, 0.406],
                std=[0.229, 0.224, 0.225])
])
```

**Apply heavy aug to train, minimal to test.**

---

# FoodVision Mini Project: Building a Custom Image Classifier

We'll use the **Food-101** dataset (subset of 10 classes).

## Step 1: Download Data

bash
```bash
# In terminal
wget https://data.vision.ee.ethz.ch/cvl/food-101.tar.gz
tar -xzf food-101.tar.gz
```

Structure:

```text
food-101/
  images/
    pizza/
    steak/
    ...
  meta/
    train.txt
    test.txt
```

---

## Step 2: Custom Dataset

```python
from torchvision import datasets, transforms
from torch.utils.data import DataLoader
import os
from pathlib import Path

# Paths
DATA_PATH = Path("food-101")
IMAGE_PATH = DATA_PATH / "images"

# Map class names
class_names = ['pizza', 'steak', 'sushi', 'hamburger', 'fried_rice',
               'ramen', 'ice_cream', 'apple_pie', 'chicken_wings',
'donuts']

# Custom dataset from folders
train_data = datasets.ImageFolder(
    IMAGE_PATH,
    transform=train_transform,
    target_transform=None,
    is_valid_file=lambda x: any(c in x for c in class_names)
)

# Filter only 10 classes
```

# We'll manually filter using train.txt later

**Better**: Use train.txt and test.txt to split properly.

---

## Step 3: Full Data Setup (Recommended)

python
```
from pathlib import Path
import random

def walk_through_dir(dir_path):
    for dirpath, dirnames, filenames in os.walk(dir_path):
        print(f"{len(dirnames)} dirs, {len(filenames)} images in
'{dirpath}'")

walk_through_dir(IMAGE_PATH)

# Read split files
def read_split_file(file_path):
    with open(file_path) as f:
        lines = [line.strip() for line in f.readlines()]
    return lines

train_files = read_split_file(DATA_PATH / "meta" / "train.txt")
test_files = read_split_file(DATA_PATH / "meta" / "test.txt")

# Filter 10 classes
selected_classes = class_names
train_files = [f for f in train_files if f.split('/')[0] in
selected_classes]
test_files = [f for f in test_files if f.split('/')[0] in selected_classes]

# Limit to 100 images per class (Mini version)
random.seed(42)
train_files = random.sample(train_files, 1000)
test_files = random.sample(test_files, 250)
```

```
# Custom dataset class
from torch.utils.data import Dataset
from PIL import Image

class FoodMiniDataset(Dataset):
    def __init__(self, files, root_dir, transform=None):
        self.files = files
        self.root_dir = root_dir
        self.transform = transform
        self.class_to_idx = {cls: idx for idx, cls in
enumerate(selected_classes)}

    def __len__(self):
        return len(self.files)

    def __getitem__(self, idx):
        img_name = self.files[idx]
        img_path = self.root_dir / "images" / (img_name + ".jpg")
        image = Image.open(img_path).convert("RGB")
        label = self.class_to_idx[img_name.split('/')[0]]

        if self.transform:
            image = self.transform(image)

        return image, label

# Create datasets
train_dataset = FoodMiniDataset(train_files, DATA_PATH,
train_transform)
test_dataset = FoodMiniDataset(test_files, DATA_PATH,
test_transform)

# DataLoaders
BATCH_SIZE = 32
train_loader = DataLoader(train_dataset,
batch_size=BATCH_SIZE, shuffle=True)
test_loader = DataLoader(test_dataset,
batch_size=BATCH_SIZE, shuffle=False)
```

## Training the CNN

python

```
# Device
device = "cuda" if torch.cuda.is_available() else "cpu"

# Model
model = TinyCNN(input_channels=3,
num_classes=len(class_names)).to(device)

# Loss & Optimizer
loss_fn = nn.CrossEntropyLoss()
optimizer = torch.optim.Adam(model.parameters(), lr=0.001)

# Training Loop
EPOCHS = 10
for epoch in range(EPOCHS):
  model.train()
  train_loss, train_acc = 0, 0
  for X, y in train_loader:
    X, y = X.to(device), y.to(device)

    logits = model(X)
    loss = loss_fn(logits, y)

    optimizer.zero_grad()
    loss.backward()
    optimizer.step()

    train_loss += loss.item()
    train_acc += (logits.argmax(dim=1) == y).sum().item()

  train_loss /= len(train_loader)
  train_acc /= len(train_loader.dataset)

  # Evaluation
  model.eval()
```

```python
    test_loss, test_acc = 0, 0
    with torch.inference_mode():
        for X, y in test_loader:
            X, y = X.to(device), y.to(device)
            logits = model(X)
            loss = loss_fn(logits, y)
            test_loss += loss.item()
            test_acc += (logits.argmax(dim=1) == y).sum().item()

    test_loss /= len(test_loader)
    test_acc /= len(test_loader.dataset)

    print(f"Epoch {epoch+1} | Train Loss: {train_loss:.4f}, Acc:
{train_acc:.4f} | Test Loss: {test_loss:.4f}, Acc: {test_acc:.4f}")
```

**Expected**: ~70–75% accuracy with TinyCNN.

---

# Transfer Learning Teaser: Fine-Tuning Pre-Trained CNNs

Training from scratch is slow and needs **thousands of images**.

**Transfer Learning** = use a model pre-trained on **ImageNet (1.4M images)**.

## Use torchvision.models

python

```python
from torchvision import models

# Load EfficientNet-B0
weights = models.EfficientNet_B0_Weights.DEFAULT
model = models.efficientnet_b0(weights=weights).to(device)
```

```
# Freeze feature extractor
for param in model.features.parameters():
    param.requires_grad = False

# Replace classifier head
import torch.nn as nn
model.classifier = nn.Sequential(
    nn.Dropout(p=0.2),
    nn.Linear(1280, len(class_names))
).to(device)

# Use same transforms as pre-trained model
auto_transforms = weights.transforms()
# Update train_transform to use auto_transforms
```

### Train Only the Head

python
```
optimizer = torch.optim.Adam(model.classifier.parameters(),
lr=0.001)
```

> **Result**: **>90% accuracy** in 5 epochs with 1000 images.

---

## Evaluation: Confusion Matrices, Precision-Recall, and Visualization

### 1. Confusion Matrix

python
```
from sklearn.metrics import confusion_matrix
import seaborn as sns
import numpy as np

model.eval()
```

```
all_preds, all_labels = [], []
with torch.inference_mode():
    for X, y in test_loader:
        X = X.to(device)
        logits = model(X)
        preds = logits.argmax(dim=1).cpu().numpy()
        all_preds.extend(preds)
        all_labels.extend(y.numpy())

cm = confusion_matrix(all_labels, all_preds)
plt.figure(figsize=(10, 8))
sns.heatmap(cm, annot=True, fmt="d",
xticklabels=class_names, yticklabels=class_names)
plt.xlabel("Predicted")
plt.ylabel("True")
plt.show()
```

---

## 2. Precision, Recall, F1

python

```
from sklearn.metrics import classification_report
print(classification_report(all_labels, all_preds,
target_names=class_names))
```

---

## 3. Visualize Predictions

python

```
def unnormalize(tensor):
    mean = torch.tensor([0.485, 0.456, 0.406])
    std = torch.tensor([0.229, 0.224, 0.225])
    tensor = tensor * std[:, None, None] + mean[:, None, None]
    return tensor.clamp(0, 1)

model.eval()
images, labels = next(iter(test_loader))
images = images.to(device)
logits = model(images)
```

```
preds = logits.argmax(dim=1)

fig, axes = plt.subplots(3, 3, figsize=(12, 12))
for i, ax in enumerate(axes.flat):
   img = unnormalize(images[i].cpu()).permute(1, 2, 0)
   ax.imshow(img)
   ax.set_title(f"Pred: {class_names[preds[i]]}\nTrue:
{class_names[labels[i]]}")
   ax.axis("off")
plt.show()
```

---

# Hands-On: Full FoodVision Mini Script

python

```
# foodvision_mini.py
import torch
import torch.nn as nn
from torchvision import models, transforms
from torch.utils.data import DataLoader
from pathlib import Path
import random
from PIL import Image
import matplotlib.pyplot as plt
from sklearn.metrics import confusion_matrix,
classification_report
import seaborn as sns
import numpy as np

# 1. Setup
device = "cuda" if torch.cuda.is_available() else "cpu"
DATA_PATH = Path("food-101")
class_names = ['pizza', 'steak', 'sushi', 'hamburger', 'fried_rice',
           'ramen', 'ice_cream', 'apple_pie', 'chicken_wings',
'donuts']

# 2. Data
```

```
def read_split(file_path):
    with open(file_path) as f:
        return [line.strip() for line in f.readlines()]

train_files = read_split(DATA_PATH / "meta" / "train.txt")
test_files = read_split(DATA_PATH / "meta" / "test.txt")
train_files = [f for f in train_files if f.split('/')[0] in class_names]
test_files = [f for f in test_files if f.split('/')[0] in class_names]
random.seed(42)
train_files = random.sample(train_files, 750)
test_files = random.sample(test_files, 250)

weights = models.EfficientNet_B0_Weights.DEFAULT
transform = weights.transforms()

class FoodDataset(torch.utils.data.Dataset):
    def __init__(self, files, transform):
        self.files = files
        self.transform = transform
        self.class_to_idx = {c: i for i, c in enumerate(class_names)}

    def __len__(self): return len(self.files)
    def __getitem__(self, idx):
        path = DATA_PATH / "images" / (self.files[idx] + ".jpg")
        img = Image.open(path).convert("RGB")
        label = self.class_to_idx[self.files[idx].split('/')[0]]
        if self.transform:
            img = self.transform(img)
        return img, label

train_ds = FoodDataset(train_files, transform)
test_ds = FoodDataset(test_files, transform)
train_loader = DataLoader(train_ds, batch_size=32,
shuffle=True)
test_loader = DataLoader(test_ds, batch_size=32)

# 3. Model
model = models.efficientnet_b0(weights=weights).to(device)
for param in model.features.parameters():
    param.requires_grad = False
```

```python
model.classifier = nn.Sequential(
    nn.Dropout(0.2),
    nn.Linear(1280, len(class_names))
).to(device)

# 4. Train
loss_fn = nn.CrossEntropyLoss()
optimizer = torch.optim.Adam(model.classifier.parameters(),
lr=0.001)
EPOCHS = 5

for epoch in range(EPOCHS):
    model.train()
    for X, y in train_loader:
        X, y = X.to(device), y.to(device)
        logits = model(X)
        loss = loss_fn(logits, y)
        optimizer.zero_grad()
        loss.backward()
        optimizer.step()

    model.eval()
    correct = 0
    with torch.inference_mode():
        for X, y in test_loader:
            X, y = X.to(device), y.to(device)
            pred = model(X).argmax(1)
            correct += (pred == y).sum().item()
    acc = correct / len(test_ds)
    print(f"Epoch {epoch+1} | Test Acc: {acc:.4f}")

# 5. Save
torch.save(model.state_dict(), "foodvision_mini.pth")
```

**Run**:

bash

```bash
python foodvision_mini.py
```

---

## Common Mistakes to Avoid

| Mistake | Fix |
|---|---|
| **Wrong input size** | Use weights.transforms() |
| **Training with test aug** | No flips/rotations on test |
| **Forgetting to freeze** | param.requires_grad = False |
| **Mismatched class order** | Use class_to_idx consistently |
| **No normalization** | Use ImageNet stats |
| **Evaluating in train mode** | model.eval() + inference_mode() |

---

## Real-World Applications

| App | Model | Accuracy |
|---|---|---|
| Food Delivery | CNN | 95%+ |
| Medical Imaging | ResNet | Diagnose tumors |
| Self-Driving Cars | CNN + Segmentation | Detect lanes, signs |
| Security | Face Recognition | 99.9% |

---

## Summary: Key Takeaways

1. **CNNs** use Conv2d + pooling to extract spatial features.
2. **Data augmentation** prevents overfitting.
3. **Transfer learning** = pre-trained model + new head.
4. **FoodVision Mini** = 10-class food classifier.
5. **Evaluation** = confusion matrix, precision/recall, visualizations.
6. **EfficientNet** > custom CNN with less data.
7. **Always normalize** with ImageNet stats.
8. **Freeze base**, train head first.

---

## Practice Exercises

### Exercise 1: Add Data Augmentation

Add RandomVerticalFlip() and RandomRotation(10) to train_transform.

### Exercise 2: Try ResNet-18

Replace EfficientNet with models.resnet18.

### Exercise 3: Predict on Custom Image

```python
from PIL import Image
img = Image.open("my_pizza.jpg")
img = transform(img).unsqueeze(0).to(device)
model.eval()
with torch.inference_mode():
    pred = model(img).argmax(1)
```

```python
print(class_names[pred])
```

---

## Challenge: "FoodVision Pro Teaser"

1. Use **all 101 classes**.
2. Train **EfficientNet-B2**.
3. Achieve **>60% top-1 accuracy**.
4. Deploy with **Gradio**.

```python
import gradio as gr
# Your interface here
```

---

**Next Chapter**: *Custom Datasets and Going Modular*

You'll build **reusable, production-ready code**.

Your model can now **see**. Feed it the world.

# Chapter 5

# Custom Datasets in PyTorch – Tailoring Data for Your Projects

In this chapter, you'll learn how to **build custom data pipelines** that work with **any data format**—from personal photo albums to CSV logs, video frames, or sensor streams.

You'll create a **fully reusable Dataset and DataLoader** for your own images, apply **professional-grade preprocessing**, and ensure **reproducibility** and **efficiency** in training.

By the end, you'll be able to:

- Write a Dataset class from scratch.
- Build **transform pipelines** with torchvision.transforms.
- Load **CSV**, **images**, **videos**, and **mixed data**.
- Use **batching**, **shuffling**, and **parallel workers**.
- Avoid **data leakage** and ensure **reproducible results**.
- Load and preprocess **your own photo collection**.

Let's turn your data into fuel for neural networks.

---

# Creating PyTorch Datasets and DataLoaders from Scratch

PyTorch's Dataset and DataLoader are the **standard way** to feed data into models.

## Core Concepts

| Component | Role |
|---|---|
| Dataset | Stores data + labels, implements __len__ and __getitem__ |
| DataLoader | Batches, shuffles, loads in parallel |

---

## Minimal Dataset Example

python
```python
from torch.utils.data import Dataset
import torch

class SimpleDataset(Dataset):
    def __init__(self, data, labels):
        self.data = data      # List or tensor
        self.labels = labels

    def __len__(self):
        return len(self.data)

    def __getitem__(self, idx):
        x = self.data[idx]
        y = self.labels[idx]
        return x, y

# Usage
```

```
data = torch.randn(100, 3, 224, 224)
labels = torch.randint(0, 10, (100,))
dataset = SimpleDataset(data, labels)
```

---

### With DataLoader

python

```
from torch.utils.data import DataLoader

loader = DataLoader(
    dataset,
    batch_size=8,
    shuffle=True,
    num_workers=2,
    pin_memory=True  # Faster CPU → GPU transfer
)

for X_batch, y_batch in loader:
    print(X_batch.shape, y_batch.shape)
    break
# Output: torch.Size([8, 3, 224, 224]) torch.Size([8])
```

> **Actionable Step**: Always set num_workers > 0 on multi-core machines.

---

## Image Transformations: Resizing, Normalization, and Custom Pipelines

Transforms convert raw data → model-ready tensors.

## Basic Transforms

python
```
from torchvision import transforms

transform = transforms.Compose([
    transforms.Resize((224, 224)),
    transforms.ToTensor(),              # [H, W, C] → [C, H, W],
/255
    transforms.Normalize(mean=[0.485, 0.456, 0.406],
                         std=[0.229, 0.224, 0.225])
])
```

---

## Train vs Test Transforms

python
```
train_transform = transforms.Compose([
    transforms.RandomResizedCrop(224),
    transforms.RandomHorizontalFlip(p=0.5),
    transforms.ColorJitter(brightness=0.2),
    transforms.ToTensor(),
    transforms.Normalize(mean=[0.485, 0.456, 0.406],
                         std=[0.229, 0.224, 0.225])
])

test_transform = transforms.Compose([
    transforms.Resize(256),
    transforms.CenterCrop(224),
    transforms.ToTensor(),
    transforms.Normalize(mean=[0.485, 0.456, 0.406],
                         std=[0.229, 0.224, 0.225])
])
```

> **Never augment test data** — it must reflect real-world input.

---

### Custom Transform (Lambda)

```python
# Add noise
add_noise = transforms.Lambda(lambda x: x +
torch.randn_like(x) * 0.1)

# Convert grayscale → RGB
to_rgb = transforms.Lambda(lambda x: x.repeat(3, 1, 1) if
x.size(0)==1 else x)
```

---

# Handling Diverse Data Formats

## 1. CSV + Images (Tabular + Vision)

```python
import pandas as pd
from PIL import Image

class CSVDataset(Dataset):
    def __init__(self, csv_file, img_dir, transform=None):
        self.df = pd.read_csv(csv_file)
        self.img_dir = Path(img_dir)
        self.transform = transform

    def __len__(self):
        return len(self.df)

    def __getitem__(self, idx):
        row = self.df.iloc[idx]
        img_path = self.img_dir / row['filename']
        image = Image.open(img_path).convert("RGB")
        label = row['label']
        features = torch.tensor(row[['age', 'height']].values,
dtype=torch.float)

        if self.transform:
```

```
        image = self.transform(image)

    return image, features, label
```

---

## 2. Video Frames

python

```
import cv2

class VideoDataset(Dataset):
    def __init__(self, video_paths, transform=None,
frames_per_clip=16):
        self.video_paths = video_paths
        self.transform = transform
        self.frames_per_clip = frames_per_clip

    def __len__(self):
        return len(self.video_paths)

    def __getitem__(self, idx):
        cap = cv2.VideoCapture(self.video_paths[idx])
        frames = []
        count = 0
        while len(frames) < self.frames_per_clip:
            ret, frame = cap.read()
            if not ret:
                break
            if count % 5 == 0:  # Sample every 5th frame
                frame = cv2.cvtColor(frame, cv2.COLOR_BGR2RGB)
                frame = Image.fromarray(frame)
                if self.transform:
                    frame = self.transform(frame)
                frames.append(frame)
            count += 1
        cap.release()

        # Stack → [T, C, H, W]
        video = torch.stack(frames)
```

```
        label = 0  # Replace with actual label
        return video, label
```

---

### 3. Mixed Modalities (Image + Text)

python
```
class MultimodalDataset(Dataset):
    def __init__(self, data, transform=None, tokenizer=None):
        self.data = data
        self.transform = transform
        self.tokenizer = tokenizer

    def __getitem__(self, idx):
        item = self.data[idx]
        image = Image.open(item['img_path']).convert("RGB")
        text = item['caption']

        if self.transform:
            image = self.transform(image)
        if self.tokenizer:
            text = self.tokenizer(text, padding="max_length",
max_length=32, truncation=True, return_tensors="pt")
            text = {k: v.squeeze(0) for k, v in text.items()}

        return image, text, item['label']
```

---

## Batching, Shuffling, and Parallel Loading

### DataLoader Parameters

| Param | Purpose |
|---|---|
| batch_size | Mini-batch size |

| | |
|---|---|
| shuffle | Randomize order each epoch |
| num_workers | Parallel data loading |
| pin_memory | Faster CPU → GPU |
| drop_last | Drop incomplete batch |

```python
loader = DataLoader(
    dataset,
    batch_size=32,
    shuffle=True,
    num_workers=4,
    pin_memory=True,
    drop_last=True
)
```

> **Pro Tip**: Use num_workers = os.cpu_count() on Linux.

---

# Hands-On: Loading and Preprocessing a Personal Photo Dataset

Let's build a **pet classifier** from your own photos.

## Folder Structure

```text
my_pets/
  train/
    cats/
      cat1.jpg
```

```
    cat2.jpg
  dogs/
    dog1.jpg
test/
  cats/
  dogs/
```

---

## Step 1: Create Dataset

python
```python
from pathlib import Path
from torchvision import datasets, transforms
from torch.utils.data import DataLoader, random_split

# Paths
DATA_PATH = Path("my_pets")
train_dir = DATA_PATH / "train"
test_dir = DATA_PATH / "test"

# Transforms
train_transform = transforms.Compose([
    transforms.Resize((224, 224)),
    transforms.RandomHorizontalFlip(),
    transforms.ToTensor(),
    transforms.Normalize(mean=[0.485, 0.456, 0.406],
                         std=[0.229, 0.224, 0.225])
])

test_transform = transforms.Compose([
    transforms.Resize((224, 224)),
    transforms.ToTensor(),
    transforms.Normalize(mean=[0.485, 0.456, 0.406],
                         std=[0.229, 0.224, 0.225])
])

# Datasets
full_train_dataset = datasets.ImageFolder(train_dir,
transform=train_transform)
```

```
test_dataset = datasets.ImageFolder(test_dir,
transform=test_transform)

# Optional: Split train → train/val
train_size = int(0.8 * len(full_train_dataset))
val_size = len(full_train_dataset) - train_size
train_dataset, val_dataset = random_split(full_train_dataset,
[train_size, val_size])

# Update val transform
val_dataset.dataset.transform = test_transform
```

---

## Step 2: DataLoaders

python

```
BATCH_SIZE = 16

train_loader = DataLoader(train_dataset,
batch_size=BATCH_SIZE, shuffle=True, num_workers=2,
pin_memory=True)
val_loader = DataLoader(val_dataset,
batch_size=BATCH_SIZE, shuffle=False, num_workers=2,
pin_memory=True)
test_loader = DataLoader(test_dataset,
batch_size=BATCH_SIZE, shuffle=False, num_workers=2,
pin_memory=True)
```

---

## Step 3: Visualize Batch

python

```
import matplotlib.pyplot as plt

def show_batch(loader):
    images, labels = next(iter(loader))
    images = images[:8]
    labels = labels[:8]
```

```
    # Unnormalize
    mean = torch.tensor([0.485, 0.456, 0.406])
    std = torch.tensor([0.229, 0.224, 0.225])
    images = images * std[:, None, None] + mean[:, None, None]
    images = images.clamp(0, 1)

    plt.figure(figsize=(12, 6))
    for i in range(8):
        plt.subplot(2, 4, i+1)
        plt.imshow(images[i].permute(1, 2, 0))
        plt.title(f"Label: {loader.dataset.dataset.classes[labels[i]]}")
        plt.axis("off")
    plt.show()

show_batch(train_loader)
```

---

# Best Practices: Avoiding Data Leaks and Ensuring Reproducibility

## 1. No Data Leakage

python

```
# WRONG: Fit normalizer on full data
scaler.fit(all_data)

# CORRECT: Fit on train only
scaler.fit(X_train)
X_val = scaler.transform(X_val)
X_test = scaler.transform(X_test)
```

---

## 2. Reproducibility

```python
import random
import numpy as np

def set_seed(seed=42):
    torch.manual_seed(seed)
    torch.cuda.manual_seed_all(seed)
    np.random.seed(seed)
    random.seed(seed)
    torch.backends.cudnn.deterministic = True
    torch.backends.cudnn.benchmark = False

set_seed(42)
```

---

## 3. Validation Set from Train

```python
train_dataset, val_dataset = random_split(
    full_dataset,
    [train_size, val_size],
    generator=torch.Generator().manual_seed(42)
)
```

---

## 4. Save Transform Pipeline

```python
import pickle
with open("train_transform.pkl", "wb") as f:
    pickle.dump(train_transform, f)
```

---

# Full Custom Dataset Script

python

```
# my_pets_classifier.py
import torch
from torch.utils.data import DataLoader, random_split
from torchvision import datasets, transforms
from pathlib import Path
import matplotlib.pyplot as plt

# 1. Setup
DATA_PATH = Path("my_pets")
train_dir = DATA_PATH / "train"
set_seed(42)

# 2. Transforms
train_transform = transforms.Compose([
    transforms.RandomResizedCrop(224),
    transforms.RandomHorizontalFlip(),
    transforms.ToTensor(),
    transforms.Normalize([0.485, 0.456, 0.406], [0.229, 0.224,
0.225])
])

test_transform = transforms.Compose([
    transforms.Resize(256),
    transforms.CenterCrop(224),
    transforms.ToTensor(),
    transforms.Normalize([0.485, 0.456, 0.406], [0.229, 0.224,
0.225])
])

# 3. Datasets
full_train = datasets.ImageFolder(train_dir,
transform=train_transform)
train_ds, val_ds = random_split(full_train, [0.8, 0.2],
generator=torch.Generator().manual_seed(42))
val_ds.dataset.transform = test_transform
```

```
test_ds = datasets.ImageFolder(DATA_PATH / "test",
transform=test_transform)

# 4. Loaders
train_loader = DataLoader(train_ds, batch_size=8,
shuffle=True, num_workers=2)
val_loader = DataLoader(val_ds, batch_size=8, shuffle=False,
num_workers=2)
test_loader = DataLoader(test_ds, batch_size=8, shuffle=False,
num_workers=2)

# 5. Test
for X, y in train_loader:
    print(X.shape, y.shape)
    break
```

---

# Common Mistakes to Avoid

| Mistake | Fix |
|---|---|
| **Augmenting test data** | Use only resize + normalize |
| **Fitting transforms on val/test** | Fit **only on train** |
| **num_workers=0 on fast CPU** | Use 2–8 workers |
| **Not setting seed** | set_seed(42) everywhere |
| **Using shuffle=True on val/test** | Only on train |
| **Forgetting pin_memory** | Add when using GPU |

---

## Real-World Applications

| Use Case | Data Type | Pipeline |
|---|---|---|
| Medical Imaging | DICOM + CSV | Custom loader |
| Autonomous Cars | Video + LiDAR | Frame sampling |
| Retail | Product images + metadata | Multimodal |
| Agriculture | Drone images + GPS | Geo-transforms |

---

## Summary: Key Takeaways

1. **Dataset** = __len__ + __getitem__
2. **DataLoader** = batching, shuffling, parallel
3. **Transforms** = Compose, Lambda, train ≠ test
4. **Handle any data**: CSV, video, mixed
5. **Avoid leakage**: Fit on train only
6. **Reproducibility**: set_seed, Generator
7. **Personal photos** → full classifier in 20 lines
8. **num_workers, pin_memory** = speed
9. **Save transforms** for inference

---

# Practice Exercises

## Exercise 1: CSV + Image Dataset

python
```
# Load: image_path, age, label from CSV
# Return: image (transformed), age (tensor), label
```

## Exercise 2: Video Frame Sampler

python
```
# Sample 8 frames uniformly from video
# Stack → [8, 3, 224, 224]
```

## Exercise 3: Custom Transform

python
```
# Add Gaussian noise only during training
class AddNoise:
    def __init__(self, std=0.1):
        self.std = std
    def __call__(self, tensor):
        return tensor + torch.randn_like(tensor) * self.std
```

---

# Challenge: "My Family Album Classifier"

1. Organize photos into family/john/, family/jane/, etc.
2. Build dataset with **age regression + name classification**.
3. Use **multimodal output**: (image) → (age, name_id)
4. Train a model with **two heads**.

python

```python
# Output: age (float), name_id (int)
```

---

**Next Chapter**: *Going Modular – Professional PyTorch Code*

You'll turn notebooks into **production-ready scripts**.

Your data is ready. Train the world.

# Chapter 6

# Going Modular – Professional PyTorch Code Organization

In this chapter, you'll **transform your Jupyter notebook experiments into clean, reusable, production-ready Python modules**—the kind of code used at **Tesla, Meta, and OpenAI**.

You'll refactor the **FoodVision Mini project** into a **modular, configurable, and version-controlled** codebase. This is what separates **hobbyists from deep learning engineers**.

By the end, you'll be able to:

- Convert notebooks → .py scripts.
- Write **training engines** with train_step, test_step.
- Use **config files** (YAML/JSON) for experiments.
- Integrate **Git** for collaboration and reproducibility.
- Build **scalable, clean code** that gets you hired.

Let's go pro.

---

# Script-Based Development: From Notebooks to Reusable Python Modules

Notebooks are great for **exploration**. Scripts are for **execution**.

## Why Scripts?

| Notebooks | Scripts |
|---|---|
| Hard to test | Easy to test |
| No CLI | python train.py --epochs 10 |
| Hidden state | Explicit flow |
| Not reusable | Import anywhere |

---

## Convert Notebook → Script

```bash
# Install
pip install nbconvert

# Convert
jupyter nbconvert --to script foodvision.ipynb
```

Then clean up:

- Remove !pip, %matplotlib inline
- Add if __name__ == "__main__":
- Split into modules

---

### Project Structure

text

```
foodvision/
├── data/
│   └── setup.py
├── models/
│   └── efficientnet.py
├── engine/
│   └── train.py
├── utils/
│   └── download_data.py
│   └── save_model.py
├── config/
│   └── config.yaml
├── train.py
├── predict.py
└── README.md
```

---

## Engine Classes: Custom Training, Testing, and Prediction Loops

Create a reusable Engine class.

### engine/train.py

python

```python
# engine/train.py
import torch
from tqdm.auto import tqdm
from typing import Dict, List, Tuple

class Engine:
    def __init__(self, model, loss_fn, optimizer, device):
        self.model = model
```

```
        self.loss_fn = loss_fn
        self.optimizer = optimizer
        self.device = device

    def train_step(self, dataloader: torch.utils.data.DataLoader)
-> Tuple[float, float]:
        self.model.train()
        train_loss, train_acc = 0, 0

        for X, y in tqdm(dataloader, desc="Training", leave=False):
            X, y = X.to(self.device), y.to(self.device)

            logits = self.model(X)
            loss = self.loss_fn(logits, y)
            train_loss += loss.item()

            self.optimizer.zero_grad()
            loss.backward()
            self.optimizer.step()

            train_acc += (logits.argmax(dim=1) == y).sum().item()

        train_loss /= len(dataloader)
        train_acc /= len(dataloader.dataset)
        return train_loss, train_acc

    def test_step(self, dataloader: torch.utils.data.DataLoader) ->
Tuple[float, float]:
        self.model.eval()
        test_loss, test_acc = 0, 0

        with torch.inference_mode():
            for X, y in tqdm(dataloader, desc="Testing",
leave=False):
                X, y = X.to(self.device), y.to(self.device)
                logits = self.model(X)
                loss = self.loss_fn(logits, y)
                test_loss += loss.item()
                test_acc += (logits.argmax(dim=1) == y).sum().item()
```

```python
        test_loss /= len(dataloader)
        test_acc /= len(dataloader.dataset)
        return test_loss, test_acc

    def train(self, train_dataloader, test_dataloader, epochs: int):
        results = {"train_loss": [], "train_acc": [], "test_loss": [],
"test_acc": []}

        for epoch in tqdm(range(epochs)):
            train_loss, train_acc = self.train_step(train_dataloader)
            test_loss, test_acc = self.test_step(test_dataloader)

            print(f"Epoch: {epoch} | Train loss: {train_loss:.4f} | Train
acc: {train_acc:.4f} | "
                  f"Test loss: {test_loss:.4f} | Test acc: {test_acc:.4f}")

            results["train_loss"].append(train_loss)
            results["train_acc"].append(train_acc)
            results["test_loss"].append(test_loss)
            results["test_acc"].append(test_acc)

        return results
```

---

# Config Files for Experiment Flexibility and Scalability

Hardcoding = bad. Configs = good.

## config/config.yaml

yaml

```yaml
data:
  name: "food101"
  num_classes: 10
  batch_size: 32
  num_workers: 2
```

```yaml
model:
  name: "efficientnet_b0"
  pretrained: true

training:
  epochs: 10
  learning_rate: 0.001
  seed: 42

paths:
  data_dir: "data/food-101"
  model_save_path: "models/foodvision_mini.pth"
```

---

## Load Config

python

```python
# utils/config.py
import yaml

def load_config(config_path: str) -> dict:
    with open(config_path, "r") as f:
        return yaml.safe_load(f)
```

---

## Use in train.py

python

```python
# train.py
import torch
from models.efficientnet import get_model
from engine.train import Engine
from data.setup import get_dataloaders
from utils.config import load_config
from utils.save_model import save_model
import argparse

def main():
    parser = argparse.ArgumentParser()
```

```
    parser.add_argument("--config", default="config/config.yaml")
    args = parser.parse_args()

    config = load_config(args.config)

    # Setup
    device = "cuda" if torch.cuda.is_available() else "cpu"
    torch.manual_seed(config["training"]["seed"])

    # Data
    train_loader, test_loader, class_names =
get_dataloaders(config)

    # Model
    model = get_model(config).to(device)

    # Engine
    loss_fn = torch.nn.CrossEntropyLoss()
    optimizer = torch.optim.Adam(model.parameters(),
lr=config["training"]["learning_rate"])
    engine = Engine(model, loss_fn, optimizer, device)

    # Train
    results = engine.train(train_loader, test_loader,
epochs=config["training"]["epochs"])

    # Save
    save_model(model, config["paths"]["model_save_path"])

if __name__ == "__main__":
    main()
```

---

# Version Control and Collaboration: Git Integration for DL Projects

## Initialize Git

bash

```
git init
git add .
git commit -m "Initial commit: FoodVision modular"
```

## .gitignore

gitignore

```
__pycache__/
*.pyc
data/
models/*.pth
.ipynb_checkpoints/
.DS_Store
env/
```

---

## Branching Strategy

bash

```
git checkout -b experiment/efficientnet-b1
# Train with different model
git add .
git commit -m "Experiment: EfficientNet-B1"
git push origin experiment/efficientnet-b1
```

---

### Track Experiments

Use **Weights & Biases**, **MLflow**, or **CSV**:

python
```
# In train.py
import csv
with open("results.csv", "a") as f:
    writer = csv.writer(f)
    writer.writerow([config["model"]["name"],
results["test_acc"][-1]])
```

---

## Hands-On Refactor: Modularizing the FoodVision Project

Let's build the full modular project.

### 1. data/setup.py

python
```
# data/setup.py
from torchvision import datasets, transforms
from torch.utils.data import DataLoader
from pathlib import Path
import random

def get_dataloaders(config):
    DATA_PATH = Path(config["paths"]["data_dir"])
    class_names = [...]  # 10 food classes

    # Transforms
    weights = torch.hub.load('pytorch/vision',
f'{config["model"]["name"]}_weights',
                        pretrained=config["model"]["pretrained"])
    transform = weights.transforms()
```

```
    # Custom dataset (same as Chapter 5)
    # ... FoodMiniDataset ...

    train_loader = DataLoader(train_dataset,
batch_size=config["data"]["batch_size"],
                              shuffle=True,
num_workers=config["data"]["num_workers"])
    test_loader = DataLoader(test_dataset,
batch_size=config["data"]["batch_size"],
                             shuffle=False,
num_workers=config["data"]["num_workers"])

    return train_loader, test_loader, class_names
```

---

## 2. models/efficientnet.py

python

```
# models/efficientnet.py
import torchvision.models as models

def get_model(config):
    model_name = config["model"]["name"]
    weights =
models.__getattribute__(f"{model_name.replace('-',
'_').upper()}_Weights").DEFAULT
    model =
models.__getattribute__(model_name)(weights=weights)

    # Replace classifier
    if "efficientnet" in model_name:
        model.classifier[1] =
torch.nn.Linear(model.classifier[1].in_features,
config["data"]["num_classes"])
    elif "resnet" in model_name:
        model.fc = torch.nn.Linear(model.fc.in_features,
config["data"]["num_classes"])

    return model
```

### 3. utils/save_model.py

python
```
# utils/save_model.py
def save_model(model, path):
   import os
   os.makedirs(os.path.dirname(path), exist_ok=True)
   torch.save(model.state_dict(), path)
   print(f"Model saved to {path}")
```

### 4. predict.py

python
```
# predict.py
import torch
from models.efficientnet import get_model
from utils.config import load_config
from PIL import Image
import torchvision.transforms as transforms

def predict(image_path, config_path="config/config.yaml"):
   config = load_config(config_path)
   device = "cuda" if torch.cuda.is_available() else "cpu"

   model = get_model(config).to(device)

model.load_state_dict(torch.load(config["paths"]["model_save_
path"]))
   model.eval()

   transform = transforms.Compose([
      transforms.Resize(256),
      transforms.CenterCrop(224),
      transforms.ToTensor(),
      transforms.Normalize([0.485, 0.456, 0.406], [0.229, 0.224,
0.225])
   ])
```

```
    img = Image.open(image_path).convert("RGB")
    img = transform(img).unsqueeze(0).to(device)

    with torch.inference_mode():
        pred = model(img).argmax(dim=1).item()

    return config["data"]["class_names"][pred]
```

**Run**:

```bash
python train.py --config config/config.yaml
python predict.py pizza.jpg
```

---

# Career Boost: Writing Production-Ready Code Employers Love

## What Recruiters Look For

| Skill | Proof |
|---|---|
| Clean code | Modular, documented |
| Reproducibility | Config + seed |
| CLI | argparse |
| Testing | unittest |
| Logging | print → logging |
| Git | Clean history |

---

### Add Logging

python
```python
import logging
logging.basicConfig(level=logging.INFO)
logger = logging.getLogger(__name__)

logger.info(f"Epoch {epoch} | Acc: {acc}")
```

---

### Add Tests

python
```python
# tests/test_model.py
def test_model_output_shape():
    model = get_model(config)
    x = torch.randn(1, 3, 224, 224)
    assert model(x).shape == (1, 10)
```

bash
```bash
pytest tests/
```

---

## Common Mistakes to Avoid

| Mistake | Fix |
|---|---|
| **Hardcoding paths** | Use config |
| **Global variables** | Pass as args |
| **No __main__ guard** | if __name__ == "__main__": |
| **Not committing config** | git add config/ |
| **No docstrings** | Add to every function |
| **Print debugging** | Use logging |

## Real-World Applications

| Company | Practice |
|---|---|
| **Tesla** | Modular training scripts, Git + CI/CD |
| **Hugging Face** | transformers library: config-driven |
| **Meta AI** | PyTorch Lightning → modular by design |

## Summary: Key Takeaways

1. **Scripts > Notebooks** for production.
2. **Modular structure**: data/, models/, engine/, utils/.
3. **Engine class** = reusable train/test loops.
4. **Config files** = experiment flexibility.
5. **Git** = version control, branching, .gitignore.
6. **CLI** with argparse.
7. **Logging, testing, docstrings** = professional code.
8. **FoodVision** now fully modular and scalable.

## Practice Exercises

### Exercise 1: Add Validation Loop

Update Engine to include val_dataloader.

### Exercise 2: Config for Learning Rate Scheduler

yaml
```yaml
scheduler:
  type: "step"
  step_size: 5
  gamma: 0.1
```

### Exercise 3: Add predict.py CLI

bash
```bash
python predict.py --image pizza.jpg --config config.yaml
```

---

## Challenge: "Experiment Tracker"

1. Add **Weights & Biases** logging.
2. Log config, metrics, model.
3. Compare two runs: efficientnet_b0 vs resnet50.

python
```python
import wandb
wandb.init(project="foodvision", config=config)
wandb.watch(model)
```

---

**Next Chapter**: *Transfer Learning Mastery*

You'll fine-tune **state-of-the-art models** in 5 lines.

Your code is now **engineer-grade**. Ship it.

# Chapter 7

# Transfer Learning Mastery – Leveraging Pre-Trained Models

In this chapter, you'll **master transfer learning**—the secret weapon that lets you build **state-of-the-art models with little data and compute**.

You'll train a **Pizza vs. Steak classifier** from just **150 images per class** and achieve **>98% accuracy** using **pre-trained models** like **EfficientNet** and **ResNet**.

By the end, you'll be able to:

- Choose between **feature extraction** and **fine-tuning**.
- Use **ResNet**, **EfficientNet**, and **Vision Transformers**.
- Adapt models to **custom domains**.
- Tune **hyperparameters** like a pro.
- Build **ensembles** that beat single models.
- Deploy **production-grade vision models**.

Let's unlock the power of pre-trained weights.

---

# Feature Extraction vs. Fine-Tuning: Choosing the Right Approach

**Transfer learning** = take a model trained on a large dataset (like **ImageNet**) and **reuse its knowledge** for your task.

### Two Strategies

| Strategy | What You Do | When to Use |
|---|---|---|
| **Feature Extraction** | Freeze base layers → train only classifier head | Small dataset (<1k images), limited compute |
| **Fine-Tuning** | Unfreeze some/all base layers → train everything | Larger dataset (>10k), want max accuracy |

---

### Feature Extraction Example

python
```
import torchvision.models as models

# Load pre-trained EfficientNet
weights = models.EfficientNet_B0_Weights.DEFAULT
model = models.efficientnet_b0(weights=weights)

# Freeze all layers
for param in model.features.parameters():
    param.requires_grad = False

# Replace classifier
model.classifier = torch.nn.Sequential(
    torch.nn.Dropout(p=0.2),
```

```
    torch.nn.Linear(1280, 2)  # Pizza vs Steak
)
```

> **Actionable Step**: Always freeze first, train head, then fine-tune if needed.

---

# Popular Architectures: ResNet, EfficientNet, and Vision Transformers

## 1. ResNet (Residual Network)

- **Skip connections** fix vanishing gradients.
- Variants: resnet18, resnet50, resnet101

python
```
model =
models.resnet50(weights=models.ResNet50_Weights.DEFAULT)
model.fc = torch.nn.Linear(2048, 2)
```

---

## 2. EfficientNet

- **Compound scaling**: depth, width, resolution.
- **EfficientNet-B0 to B7** → B0 fastest, B7 most accurate.

python
```
model =
models.efficientnet_b0(weights=models.EfficientNet_B0_Weights.DEFAULT)
model.classifier[1] = torch.nn.Linear(1280, 2)
```

### 3. Vision Transformers (ViT)

- Split image into **patches**, treat like tokens.
- Pre-trained on **ImageNet-21k**.

python
```
model =
models.vit_b_16(weights=models.ViT_B_16_Weights.DEFAUL
T)
model.heads.head = torch.nn.Linear(768, 2)
```

> **Use EfficientNet-B0** for speed + accuracy balance.

---

# Domain Adaptation: Adapting Models to New Tasks and Datasets

Your data ≠ ImageNet. **Domain gap** exists.

## Fixes

| Problem | Solution |
|---|---|
| Different resolution | Use model's transforms() |
| Different distribution | Add **augmentation** |
| Different classes | Replace **head** |

python
```
# Use exact transforms from pre-training
weights = models.EfficientNet_B0_Weights.DEFAULT
transform = weights.transforms()  # 224x224, ImageNet stats
```

# Hyperparameter Tuning for Optimal Performance

## Key Hyperparameters

| Param | Typical Values |
|---|---|
| batch_size | 16, 32, 64 |
| learning_rate | 1e-3 (head), 1e-5 (fine-tune) |
| epochs | 5–20 |
| weight_decay | 1e-5 |

## Learning Rate Scheduling

python
```
scheduler = torch.optim.lr_scheduler.StepLR(optimizer,
step_size=3, gamma=0.1)
# Reduce LR every 3 epochs
```

## Early Stopping

python
```
best_acc = 0
patience = 3
wait = 0

for epoch in range(epochs):
    # train/test
    if val_acc > best_acc:
```

```
        best_acc = val_acc
        wait = 0
        torch.save(model.state_dict(), "best_model.pth")
    else:
        wait += 1
        if wait >= patience:
            print("Early stopping!")
            break
```

---

# Hands-On: Transfer Learning on a Custom Pizza vs. Steak Classifier

We'll use **Daniel Bourke's dataset** (150 pizza, 150 steak images).

## Step 1: Download Data

bash

```
wget
https://github.com/mrdbourke/pytorch-deep-learning/raw/main/data/pizza_steak_sushi.zip
unzip pizza_steak_sushi.zip -d data/
```

Structure:

text

```
data/pizza_steak_sushi/
  train/
    pizza/
    steak/
  test/
    pizza/
    steak/
```

---

## Step 2: Full Training Script

python
```
# pizza_steak_classifier.py
import torch
import torch.nn as nn
from torchvision import models, transforms
from torch.utils.data import DataLoader
from torchvision.datasets import ImageFolder
from engine.train import Engine  # From Chapter 6
import argparse

def main():
    parser = argparse.ArgumentParser()
    parser.add_argument("--model", default="efficientnet_b0")
    parser.add_argument("--epochs", type=int, default=10)
    parser.add_argument("--batch_size", type=int, default=32)
    parser.add_argument("--lr", type=float, default=0.001)
    args = parser.parse_args()

    # Device
    device = "cuda" if torch.cuda.is_available() else "cpu"

    # Data
    weights = getattr(models, f"{args.model}_weights", None)
    if weights is None:
        weights = models.EfficientNet_B0_Weights.DEFAULT
        model_fn = models.efficientnet_b0
    else:
        weights = weights.DEFAULT
        model_fn = getattr(models, args.model)

    transform = weights.transforms()

    train_data = ImageFolder("data/pizza_steak_sushi/train",
transform=transform)
    test_data = ImageFolder("data/pizza_steak_sushi/test",
transform=transform)
```

```
    train_loader = DataLoader(train_data,
batch_size=args.batch_size, shuffle=True, num_workers=2)
    test_loader = DataLoader(test_data,
batch_size=args.batch_size, shuffle=False, num_workers=2)

    # Model
    model = model_fn(weights=weights).to(device)

    # Freeze base
    for param in model.features.parameters():
        param.requires_grad = False

    # Replace head
    if "efficientnet" in args.model:
        model.classifier[1] =
nn.Linear(model.classifier[1].in_features, 2)
    elif "resnet" in args.model:
        model.fc = nn.Linear(model.fc.in_features, 2)
    elif "vit" in args.model:
        model.heads.head =
nn.Linear(model.heads.head.in_features, 2)

    # Loss & Optimizer
    loss_fn = nn.CrossEntropyLoss()
    optimizer = torch.optim.Adam(model.parameters(), lr=args.lr)

    # Engine
    engine = Engine(model, loss_fn, optimizer, device)
    results = engine.train(train_loader, test_loader,
epochs=args.epochs)

    # Save
    torch.save(model.state_dict(),
f"models/{args.model}_pizza_steak.pth")

if __name__ == "__main__":
    main()
```

**Run**:

bash
```
python pizza_steak_classifier.py --model efficientnet_b0
--epochs 5
```

**Expected**: **>98% test accuracy in 5 epochs**

---

## Advanced: Ensemble Methods and Model Stacking

One model = good. **Multiple models = better**.

### 1. Simple Averaging

python
```
model1 = load_model("efficientnet_b0.pth")
model2 = load_model("resnet50.pth")

def ensemble_predict(img):
    with torch.inference_mode():
        out1 = model1(img)
        out2 = model2(img)
        return (out1 + out2).argmax(dim=1)
```

---

### 2. Weighted Ensemble

python
```
# EfficientNet: 0.7, ResNet: 0.3
pred = 0.7 * out1 + 0.3 * out2
```

---

### 3. Stacking (Meta-Learner)

python
```
# Train logistic regression on model outputs
```

```python
from sklearn.linear_model import LogisticRegression

train_preds = np.hstack([model1_preds, model2_preds])
stacker = LogisticRegression()
stacker.fit(train_preds, y_train)
```

---

# Evaluation: Beyond Accuracy

## Confusion Matrix

python
```python
from sklearn.metrics import confusion_matrix
import seaborn as sns

# Get predictions
model.eval()
preds, trues = [], []
with torch.inference_mode():
    for X, y in test_loader:
        X = X.to(device)
        pred = model(X).argmax(1).cpu()
        preds.extend(pred)
        trues.extend(y)

cm = confusion_matrix(trues, preds)
sns.heatmap(cm, annot=True, xticklabels=["Pizza", "Steak"],
yticklabels=["Pizza", "Steak"])
```

---

## Classification Report

python
```python
from sklearn.metrics import classification_report
print(classification_report(trues, preds, target_names=["Pizza",
"Steak"]))
```

---

## Common Mistakes to Avoid

| Mistake | Fix |
|---|---|
| **Not using model transforms** | weights.transforms() |
| **Fine-tuning too early** | Train head first |
| **Forgetting to freeze** | param.requires_grad = False |
| **Mismatched input size** | Resize to 224 |
| **No early stopping** | Save best model |
| **Evaluating in train mode** | model.eval() |

---

## Real-World Applications

| Task | Model | Data | Accuracy |
|---|---|---|---|
| Skin Cancer Detection | EfficientNet | 10k derm images | 94% |
| Plant Disease | ResNet50 | 50k leaves | 99% |
| Food Recognition | ViT | 100k plates | 92% |
| Satellite Imaging | EfficientNet-B7 | 1M tiles | 97% |

---

## Summary: Key Takeaways

1. **Transfer learning** = reuse ImageNet weights.
2. **Feature extraction** = freeze base, train head.
3. **Fine-tuning** = unfreeze later for max accuracy.
4. **EfficientNet** = best speed/accuracy.
5. **Use weights.transforms()** always.
6. **Hyperparameters**: lr, batch_size, scheduler.
7. **Pizza vs Steak** = 98% in 5 epochs.
8. **Ensembles** > single models.
9. **Evaluate** with confusion matrix, precision/recall.
10. **Production code** = modular, configurable.

---

## Practice Exercises

### Exercise 1: Try ResNet18

bash
```bash
python pizza_steak_classifier.py --model resnet18 --epochs 5
```

Compare accuracy and speed.

### Exercise 2: Fine-Tune Last Layer

python
```python
# Unfreeze last EfficientNet block
for name, param in model.named_parameters():
    if "features.8" in name:
        param.requires_grad = True
optimizer = torch.optim.Adam(filter(lambda p: p.requires_grad,
model.parameters()), lr=1e-5)
```

### Exercise 3: Predict on Custom Image

python

```
from PIL import Image
img = Image.open("my_steak.jpg")
img = transform(img).unsqueeze(0).to(device)
pred = model(img).argmax(1).item()
print("Pizza" if pred == 0 else "Steak")
```

---

## Challenge: "FoodVision Pro – 3-Class"

1. Add **Sushi** class (total 3 classes).
2. Use **EfficientNet-B0 + ResNet50 ensemble**.
3. Achieve **>97% accuracy**.
4. Deploy with **Gradio**.

python

```
import gradio as gr
def predict(img):
    # return ensemble prediction
    pass

interface = gr.Interface(fn=predict, inputs="image",
outputs="label")
interface.launch()
```

---

**Next Chapter**: *Experiment Tracking – Logging and Comparing Models*

You'll track **100+ experiments** with **Weights & Biases**.

You now beat humans at food recognition.

Time to scale.

# Chapter 8

# Experiment Tracking – Logging and Comparing Your Models

In this chapter, you'll learn **how to track, compare, and reproduce every experiment**—the **secret habit of top deep learning engineers**.

You'll log **multiple CNN variants** on the **Pizza vs. Steak** dataset using **Weights & Biases (WandB)**, visualize **training curves**, and generate **automated reports** for your portfolio.

By the end, you'll:

- Understand **why tracking is essential**.
- Use **WandB**, **TensorBoard**, and **MLflow**.
- Log **metrics**, **hyperparameters**, **models**, and **artifacts**.
- Run **ablation studies** and compare models.
- Build a **professional experiment dashboard**.
- Automate **portfolio-ready reports**.

Let's make your experiments **repeatable, comparable, and shareable**.

---

# Why Track? Reproducibility, Iteration, and Team Collaboration

Without tracking, you **forget**:

- Which model was best?
- What learning rate worked?
- Why one run failed?

## The Cost of Not Tracking

| Problem | Example |
|---|---|
| **Lost best model** | "Wait, which checkpoint had 98% accuracy?" |
| **Irreproducible results** | "It worked on my machine…" |
| **Wasted time** | Retraining the same config |
| **Team confusion** | "Did you try dropout=0.3?" |

---

## Benefits of Tracking

| Benefit | Outcome |
|---|---|
| **Reproducibility** | wandb run --recreate |
| **Iteration** | Compare 50 runs in 1 click |
| **Collaboration** | Share dashboard with team |
| **Portfolio** | Auto-generated reports |

**Real-World**: OpenAI, Meta, Tesla **track every run**.

---

## Tools Overview: Weights & Biases (WandB), TensorBoard, and MLflow

| Tool | Best For | Free Tier |
|---|---|---|
| **Weights & Biases** | Rich UI, team collab, sweeps | Yes (unlimited public) |
| **TensorBoard** | Local, PyTorch native | Free |
| **MLflow** | Enterprise, model registry | Free |

We'll use **WandB — industry standard**.

---

### Install & Login

bash

```
pip install wandb
wandb login
# Paste API key from https://wandb.ai/authorize
```

---

# Logging Metrics, Hyperparameters, and Artifacts in PyTorch

## Initialize Run

python
```
import wandb

wandb.init(
   project="foodvision",
   name="efficientnet_b0_lr0.001",
   config={
      "model": "efficientnet_b0",
      "lr": 0.001,
      "batch_size": 32,
      "epochs": 10,
      "dataset": "pizza_steak"
   }
)
```

---

## Log Metrics

python
```
for epoch in range(epochs):
   train_loss, train_acc = train_step(...)
   test_loss, test_acc = test_step(...)

   wandb.log({
      "train_loss": train_loss,
      "train_acc": train_acc,
      "test_loss": test_loss,
      "test_acc": test_acc,
      "epoch": epoch
   })
```

---

### Log Model & Artifacts

```python
# Save model
torch.save(model.state_dict(), "models/effnet_b0.pth")

# Log as artifact
artifact = wandb.Artifact("model", type="model")
artifact.add_file("models/effnet_b0.pth")
wandb.log_artifact(artifact)

# Log config
wandb.config.update({"seed": 42})
```

---

### Finish Run

```python
wandb.finish()
```

---

## Visualizing Training Curves and Ablation Studies

### Training Curves

WandB auto-plots:

- train_acc vs test_acc
- train_loss vs test_loss

---

### Ablation Study: Compare Models

| Run | Model | LR | Accuracy |
|---|---|---|---|
| 1 | EffNet-B0 | 0.001 | 98.2% |
| 2 | ResNet50 | 0.001 | 97.1% |
| 3 | EffNet-B0 | 0.0001 | 96.5% |

**WandB Table** → sort, filter, group.

---

## Hands-On Milestone Project 1: Tracking Experiments on Multiple CNN Variants

We'll train **3 models** on **Pizza vs. Steak** and compare.

### Project Structure

text
```
foodvision_experiments/
├── train.py
├── models/
├── data/
└── wandb/
```

---

### train.py with WandB

python
```
# train.py
import torch
import torch.nn as nn
from torchvision import models, transforms
```

```
from torch.utils.data import DataLoader
from torchvision.datasets import ImageFolder
from engine.train import Engine
import wandb
import argparse
import os

def main():
    parser = argparse.ArgumentParser()
    parser.add_argument("--model", type=str,
default="efficientnet_b0")
    parser.add_argument("--lr", type=float, default=0.001)
    parser.add_argument("--epochs", type=int, default=5)
    parser.add_argument("--batch_size", type=int, default=32)
    args = parser.parse_args()

    # WandB init
    run = wandb.init(
        project="foodvision-pizza-steak",
        name=f"{args.model}_lr{args.lr}",
        config=vars(args)
    )

    device = "cuda" if torch.cuda.is_available() else "cpu"

    # Data
    weights = getattr(models, f"{args.model.replace('-',
'_').upper()}_Weights", None)
    if weights:
        weights = weights.DEFAULT
    else:
        weights = models.EfficientNet_B0_Weights.DEFAULT
    transform = weights.transforms()

    train_data = ImageFolder("data/pizza_steak_sushi/train",
transform=transform)
    test_data = ImageFolder("data/pizza_steak_sushi/test",
transform=transform)
```

```
    train_loader = DataLoader(train_data,
batch_size=args.batch_size, shuffle=True, num_workers=2)
    test_loader = DataLoader(test_data,
batch_size=args.batch_size, shuffle=False, num_workers=2)

    # Model
    model_fn = getattr(models, args.model,
models.efficientnet_b0)
    model = model_fn(weights=weights).to(device)

    # Freeze base
    for param in model.features.parameters() if hasattr(model,
"features") else model.parameters():
        param.requires_grad = False

    # Replace head
    if "efficientnet" in args.model:
        in_features = model.classifier[1].in_features
        model.classifier[1] = nn.Linear(in_features, 2)
    elif "resnet" in args.model:
        model.fc = nn.Linear(model.fc.in_features, 2)

    # Training
    loss_fn = nn.CrossEntropyLoss()
    optimizer = torch.optim.Adam(model.parameters(), lr=args.lr)
    engine = Engine(model, loss_fn, optimizer, device)

    # Track gradients
    wandb.watch(model, log="all", log_freq=100)

    results = {"train_loss": [], "train_acc": [], "test_loss": [],
"test_acc": []}
    for epoch in range(args.epochs):
        train_loss, train_acc = engine.train_step(train_loader)
        test_loss, test_acc = engine.test_step(test_loader)

        wandb.log({
            "train_loss": train_loss,
            "train_acc": train_acc,
            "test_loss": test_loss,
```

```
            "test_acc": test_acc,
            "epoch": epoch
        })

        results["train_loss"].append(train_loss)
        results["train_acc"].append(train_acc)
        results["test_loss"].append(test_loss)
        results["test_acc"].append(test_acc)

    # Save model
    model_path = f"models/{run.name}.pth"
    os.makedirs("models", exist_ok=True)
    torch.save(model.state_dict(), model_path)

    # Log artifact
    artifact = wandb.Artifact("model", type="model")
    artifact.add_file(model_path)
    wandb.log_artifact(artifact)

    # Log confusion matrix
    from sklearn.metrics import confusion_matrix
    import numpy as np
    model.eval()
    preds, trues = [], []
    with torch.inference_mode():
        for X, y in test_loader:
            X = X.to(device)
            pred = model(X).argmax(1).cpu().numpy()
            preds.extend(pred)
            trues.extend(y.numpy())
    cm = confusion_matrix(trues, preds)
    wandb.log({"confusion_matrix": wandb.plot.confusion_matrix(
        probs=None, y_true=trues, preds=preds,
class_names=["Pizza", "Steak"]
    )})

    wandb.finish()

if __name__ == "__main__":
    main()
```

---

## Run Experiments

bash

```bash
# 1. EfficientNet-B0
python train.py --model efficientnet_b0 --lr 0.001

# 2. ResNet50
python train.py --model resnet50 --lr 0.001

# 3. EfficientNet-B0 with lower LR
python train.py --model efficientnet_b0 --lr 0.0001
```

---

## View Dashboard

Go to:
https://wandb.ai/your-username/foodvision-pizza-steak

You'll see:

- Training curves
- Accuracy comparison
- Confusion matrices
- Model artifacts

---

# Pro Workflow: Automating Reports for Portfolio Showcases

## 1. Auto-Report with WandB

python

```python
# At end of script
report = wandb.Api().report()
```

```python
# Or use WandB Sweeps + Reports
```

---

### 2. Export to HTML

```python
# In WandB UI → Share → Export
```

---

### 3. Portfolio Snippet

```markdown
## FoodVision: Pizza vs Steak Classifier
- **Dataset**: 300 images
- **Best Model**: EfficientNet-B0
- **Test Accuracy**: 98.7%
- **Dashboard**: [wandb.ai/link](https://wandb.ai/...)
```

---

## TensorBoard Alternative

```python
from torch.utils.tensorboard import SummaryWriter

writer = SummaryWriter(log_dir="runs/exp1")
writer.add_scalar("Loss/train", train_loss, epoch)
writer.add_scalar("Accuracy/test", test_acc, epoch)
writer.close()

# Launch
tensorboard --logdir=runs
```

---

## MLflow (Bonus)

```bash
pip install mlflow
mlflow ui
```

```python
import mlflow
mlflow.start_run()
mlflow.log_param("lr", 0.001)
mlflow.log_metric("accuracy", 0.987)
mlflow.pytorch.log_model(model, "model")
mlflow.end_run()
```

---

## Common Mistakes to Avoid

| Mistake | Fix |
|---|---|
| **Not logging config** | wandb.config.update(...) |
| **Forgetting wandb.finish()** | Always call |
| **Logging too much** | Use log_freq |
| **No run names** | name="exp1_lr0.001" |
| **Not saving model** | Log as artifact |
| **Local only** | Push to cloud |

---

## Real-World Applications

| Company | Tool |
|---|---|
| **OpenAI** | WandB + internal |
| **Tesla** | Custom + MLflow |
| **Hugging Face** | WandB + Gradio |

| FAIR | TensorBoard + PyTorch |
|---|---|

---

## Summary: Key Takeaways

1. **Track everything**: metrics, config, models.
2. **WandB** = best for teams and portfolios.
3. **Log** with wandb.log(), wandb.watch(), wandb.Artifact.
4. **Compare** runs in dashboard.
5. **Ablation studies** = systematic testing.
6. **Automate reports** for job applications.
7. **Reproducibility** = seed + config + artifact.
8. **3 CNNs tracked** → clear winner.

---

## Practice Exercises

### Exercise 1: Add Validation Set

Split train → train/val, log val_acc.

### Exercise 2: Log Images

```python
wandb.log({"examples": [wandb.Image(img) for img in batch]})
```

### Exercise 3: Try TensorBoard

Replace WandB with SummaryWriter.

---

## Challenge: "Hyperparameter Sweep"

Use **WandB Sweeps** to test:

yaml

```yaml
parameters:
  lr:
    values: [0.001, 0.0001, 0.00001]
  batch_size:
    values: [16, 32, 64]
```

Find **best combo**.

bash

```bash
wandb sweep sweep.yaml
wandb agent <sweep-id>
```

---

**Next Chapter**: *Replicating Research Papers*

You'll **reproduce a CVPR paper** from scratch.

Your experiments are now **bulletproof**.

Keep iterating.

# Chapter 9

# Replicating Research Papers – Bringing Cutting-Edge Ideas to Life

In this chapter, you'll **demystify research papers** and **reproduce a state-of-the-art (SOTA) model from scratch**—the exact skill that gets you hired at **Google, Meta, and Tesla**.

You'll replicate **YOLOv8** (You Only Look Once) for **real-time object detection** and train it on a **custom dataset** to detect **food items in images**.

By the end, you'll be able to:

- Read and **extract key ideas** from any CV/ML paper.
- **Implement SOTA models** using PyTorch.
- **Debug** replication failures.
- **Scale training** with distributed GPUs.
- Complete **Milestone Project 2**: Replicate a CVPR paper.
- **Publish your findings** on GitHub and arXiv.

Let's turn theory into working code.

---

# Reading and Breaking Down ML Papers: Structure and Key Insights

Most papers follow this **standard structure**:

| Section | What to Look For |
|---|---|
| **Abstract** | One-sentence summary |
| **Introduction** | Problem, contribution, results |
| **Related Work** | What others did |
| **Method** | **The gold** — architecture, loss, training |
| **Experiments** | Datasets, metrics, ablation |
| **Results** | Tables, graphs |
| **Conclusion** | Takeaways, limitations |

---

## How to Read a Paper (30-Minute Rule)

```text
1. Read Title + Abstract → 2 min
2. Skim Introduction → 3 min
3. Look at Figures/Tables → 5 min
4. Read Method (focus on architecture) → 15 min
5. Check Experiments (dataset, metrics) → 5 min
```

**Goal**: Can you **re-implement** in <1 week?

---

### Example: YOLOv8 Paper (Ultralytics, 2023)

- **Task**: Real-time object detection
- **Key Ideas**:
  - Anchor-free
  - Mosaic augmentation
  - C2f backbone
  - PAN neck
  - Task-aligned assigner
- **Metrics**: mAP@50-95 on COCO
- **Code**: Open-source → github.com/ultralytics/ultralytics

---

# Implementing State-of-the-Art Models: YOLO for Object Detection Example

We'll **build YOLOv8-nano** from scratch in PyTorch.

### Install YOLOv8

bash
```
pip install ultralytics
```

### Use Pretrained Model

python
```
from ultralytics import YOLO

# Load pretrained YOLOv8n
model = YOLO("yolov8n.pt")  # nano version

# Predict
results = model("pizza.jpg")
```

```python
results[0].show()  # Opens image with boxes
```

---

## Train on Custom Data

### 1. Dataset Format (YOLO style)

text
```
data/food_detection/
├── images/
│   ├── train/
│   ├── val/
├── labels/
│   ├── train/
│   ├── val/
data.yaml
```

data.yaml:

yaml
```yaml
train: ./food_detection/images/train
val: ./food_detection/images/val
nc: 3
names: ['pizza', 'burger', 'sushi']
```

### 2. Label Format (per image)

labels/train/img1.txt:

text
```
0 0.5 0.5 0.3 0.4    # class_id center_x center_y width height
(normalized)
```

---

### 3. Train

python
```python
# train_yolo.py
from ultralytics import YOLO
```

```python
model = YOLO("yolov8n.pt")  # or yolov8s.pt, yolov8m.pt

results = model.train(
    data="data.yaml",
    epochs=50,
    imgsz=640,
    batch=16,
    name="food_yolov8n"
)
```

**Output**:

text

```
Results saved to runs/detect/food_yolov8n
Best model: runs/detect/food_yolov8n/weights/best.pt
```

---

#### 4. Evaluate

python

```python
metrics = model.val()
print(metrics.box.map)  # mAP@50-95
```

---

#### 5. Inference

python

```python
model = YOLO("runs/detect/food_yolov8n/weights/best.pt")
results = model("test_images/burger_plate.jpg")
results[0].show()
```

---

## Debugging Replications: Common Pitfalls and Validation Techniques

| Pitfall | Fix |
|---|---|
| **Wrong data format** | Use ultralytics.data.utils.check_dataset() |
| **Mismatched image/label names** | img1.jpg ↔ img1.txt |
| **Incorrect normalization** | YOLO uses img / 255 |
| **No augmentation** | Enable Mosaic, MixUp |
| **Overfitting** | Use val set, early stopping |
| **GPU OOM** | Reduce batch, imgsz=416 |

---

### Validation Script

python
```
from ultralytics.utils.checks import check_dataset
check_dataset("data.yaml")
```

---

## Scaling Up: Distributed Training and Larger Datasets

### Use Multiple GPUs

python
```
model.train(
```

```
    data="data.yaml",
    epochs=100,
    batch=64,
    device=0,1  # GPU 0 and 1
)
```

### Larger Dataset: COCO8

yaml

```yaml
train: ./coco8/images/train
val: ./coco8/images/val
nc: 80
names: [...]  # COCO classes
```

bash

```bash
wget https://ultralytics.com/assets/coco8.zip
unzip coco8.zip
```

---

# Hands-On Milestone Project 2: Replicating a SOTA Computer Vision Paper

**Paper**: *YOLOv8: Real-Time Object Detection* (2023)

**Goal**: Replicate on **custom food dataset** with **3 classes**.

---

### Step 1: Prepare Dataset

bash

```bash
# Create structure
mkdir -p food_detection/{images,labels}/{train,val}

# Copy 100 images per class → train
# 20 images per class → val
```

# Convert bounding boxes to YOLO format

Use **LabelImg** or **Roboflow**:

```bash
pip install labelImg
labelImg
```

---

## Step 2: data.yaml

```yaml
train: ./food_detection/images/train
val: ./food_detection/images/val
nc: 3
names: ['pizza', 'burger', 'sushi']
```

---

## Step 3: Train YOLOv8-nano

```python
# milestone_yolo.py
from ultralytics import YOLO
import wandb

wandb.init(project="food-detection", name="yolov8n-food")

model = YOLO("yolov8n.pt")

results = model.train(
    data="data.yaml",
    epochs=100,
    imgsz=640,
    batch=32,
    name="yolov8n_food",
    patience=20,  # early stopping
    project="food-detection"
)
```

```
wandb.finish()
```

---

### Step 4: Evaluate

```python
metrics = model.val()
print(f"mAP@50: {metrics.box.map50:.3f}")
print(f"mAP@50-95: {metrics.box.map:.3f}")
```

**Target**: **mAP@50 > 0.85**

---

### Step 5: Export & Deploy

```python
# Export to ONNX
model.export(format="onnx")

# Or TorchScript
model.export(format="torchscript")
```

---

## From Theory to Impact: Publishing Your Own Findings

### 1. GitHub Repo

```text
food-yolov8/
├── data.yaml
├── train.py
├── results/
│   └── runs/detect/yolov8n_food/
├── README.md
└── report.pdf
```

### 2. Write a Report

markdown

```
# FoodYOLO: Real-Time Food Detection

## Abstract
Trained YOLOv8 on 360 custom food images → **mAP@50 =
0.91**

## Method
- YOLOv8-nano
- 640x640, 100 epochs
- Mosaic, MixUp, HSV aug

## Results
| Model | mAP@50 | mAP@50-95 |
|-------|--------|-----------|
| YOLOv8n | 0.91 | 0.67 |

## Demo
![demo](results/prediction.jpg)
```

### 3. Share

- GitHub: github.com/yourname/food-yolov8
- Hugging Face Spaces
- arXiv (optional)

---

# Common Mistakes to Avoid

| Mistake | Fix |
|---|---|
| **Wrong label format** | Use class x_center y_center w h |
| **No validation split** | Always have val/ |

| | |
|---|---|
| **Training on test data** | Never touch test set |
| **Ignoring warnings** | Run check_dataset() |
| **No version control** | git commit -m "YOLOv8 food train" |
| **Not saving best model** | model.train(..., patience=20) |

---

## Real-World Applications

| Use Case | Model | Impact |
|---|---|---|
| **Tesla FSD** | Custom YOLO | Detect cars, pedestrians |
| **Amazon Go** | YOLO | Track items in store |
| **Medical Imaging** | YOLO | Detect tumors in X-rays |
| **Agriculture** | YOLO | Count fruits on trees |

---

## Summary: Key Takeaways

1. **Read papers** in 30 minutes: focus on **Method** and **Experiments**.
2. **YOLOv8** = SOTA real-time detection.
3. **Custom data** → YOLO format → data.yaml.
4. **Train** with model.train(data=...).
5. **Debug** with check_dataset(), val split.
6. **Scale** with multi-GPU, larger data.

7. **Milestone 2**: YOLOv8 on food → **mAP@50 > 0.85**.
8. **Publish** on GitHub + report.
9. **Reproducibility** = code + data + config.

---

# Practice Exercises

## Exercise 1: Add New Class

Add **sushi roll** → retrain → compare mAP.

## Exercise 2: Try YOLOv8s

python

```
model = YOLO("yolov8s.pt")
```

Is it worth the speed/accuracy trade-off?

## Exercise 3: Export to ONNX

python

```
model.export(format="onnx")
# Test with OpenCV
```

---

# Challenge: "Replicate DETR"

**Paper**: *DETR: End-to-End Object Detection with Transformers* (Facebook, 2020)

1. Implement **DETR-ResNet50** from scratch.
2. Train on **COCO8**.
3. Achieve **mAP > 0.3**.
4. Compare with YOLOv8.

```python
# Use Hugging Face Transformers
from transformers import DetrImageProcessor,
DetrForObjectDetection
```

---

**Next Chapter**: *Model Deployment – From Code to Production AI*

You'll deploy **FoodVision** as a **live web app**.

You just reproduced **CVPR-level work**.

Now ship it.

# Chapter 10

# Model Deployment – From Code to Production AI

In this chapter, you'll **deploy your trained FoodVision model** into the **real world**—as a **live web app**, **mobile app**, **cloud API**, and **edge device**.

You'll complete **Milestone Project 3**: Deploy **FoodVision Pro** as a **fully functional web app** that classifies food in real time using your phone camera.

By the end, you'll be able to:

- Export models with **TorchScript**, **ONNX**, and **quantization**.
- Deploy with **Streamlit**, **Hugging Face Spaces**, **AWS**, and **mobile**.
- Build **secure, ethical AI** with bias checks.
- Ship **production-grade AI** that works anywhere.

Let's go live.

---

## Exporting PyTorch Models: TorchScript, ONNX, and Quantization

Your .pth file is **not enough** for production.

## 1. TorchScript

Converts model to **executable script** — no Python needed.

```python
# Save during training
torch.save(model.state_dict(), "foodvision.pth")

# Load and script
model = FoodVisionModel()
model.load_state_dict(torch.load("foodvision.pth"))
model.eval()

# Trace with example input
example = torch.randn(1, 3, 224, 224)
scripted_model = torch.jit.trace(model, example)
scripted_model.save("foodvision_scripted.pt")
```

**Run without PyTorch**:

```python
scripted = torch.jit.load("foodvision_scripted.pt")
pred = scripted(example)
```

---

## 2. ONNX (Open Neural Network Exchange)

**Universal format** — works with TensorFlow, TensorRT, OpenVINO.

```python
import torch.onnx

# Export
torch.onnx.export(
```

```
    model,
    example,
    "foodvision.onnx",
    input_names=["input"],
    output_names=["output"],
    dynamic_axes={"input": {0: "batch_size"}, "output": {0:
"batch_size"}}
)
```

**Test with ONNX Runtime**:

```python
import onnxruntime as ort
session = ort.InferenceSession("foodvision.onnx")
pred = session.run(None, {"input": example.numpy()})
```

---

## 3. Quantization (Reduce Size & Speed Up)

Convert float32 → int8 → **4x smaller, 3x faster**.

```python
# Post-training quantization
quantized_model = torch.quantization.quantize_dynamic(
    model, {torch.nn.Linear}, dtype=torch.qint8
)
torch.save(quantized_model.state_dict(),
"foodvision_quantized.pth")
```

| Format | Size | Speed | Use Case |
|---|---|---|---|
| .pth | 100 MB | Slow | Training |
| TorchScript | 95 MB | Fast | Desktop |
| ONNX | 90 MB | Faster | Cross-platform |

| Quantized | 25 MB | Fastest | Mobile/Edge |
|---|---|---|---|

---

# Web Deployment: Streamlit Apps and Hugging Face Spaces

## 1. Streamlit (Local Web App)

bash
```bash
pip install streamlit
```

python
```python
# app.py
import streamlit as st
import torch
from PIL import Image
import torchvision.transforms as T

# Load model
model = torch.jit.load("foodvision_scripted.pt")
model.eval()

# Transform
transform = T.Compose([
    T.Resize(256),
    T.CenterCrop(224),
    T.ToTensor(),
    T.Normalize([0.485, 0.456, 0.406], [0.229, 0.224, 0.225])
])

class_names = ['pizza', 'steak', 'sushi']

st.title("FoodVision Pro")
uploaded_file = st.file_uploader("Upload food image",
type=["jpg", "png"])

if uploaded_file:
```

```
img = Image.open(uploaded_file)
st.image(img, caption="Uploaded Image")

img_tensor = transform(img).unsqueeze(0)

with torch.inference_mode():
    pred = model(img_tensor).argmax(dim=1).item()

st.write(f"**Prediction: {class_names[pred].upper()}**")
```

**Run**:

bash
```
streamlit run app.py
```

---

## 2. Hugging Face Spaces (Free Public Hosting)

1. Push code to GitHub
2. Go to huggingface.co/spaces
3. Create new Space → **Streamlit**
4. Link repo → **Deploy**

**Live in 2 minutes**:
https://huggingface.co/spaces/yourname/foodvision

---

# Cloud Integration: AWS SageMaker, Google Colab, and API Endpoints

## 1. FastAPI (Local API)

python
```python
# api.py
from fastapi import FastAPI, File, UploadFile
from PIL import Image
import io
import torch

app = FastAPI()
model = torch.jit.load("foodvision_scripted.pt")
model.eval()

@app.post("/predict")
async def predict(file: UploadFile = File(...)):
    img_bytes = await file.read()
    img = Image.open(io.BytesIO(img_bytes))
    img_tensor = transform(img).unsqueeze(0)

    with torch.inference_mode():
        pred = model(img_tensor).argmax(1).item()

    return {"prediction": class_names[pred]}
```

**Run**:

bash
```bash
uvicorn api.py:api --reload
```

**Test**:

bash
```bash
curl -X POST -F "file=@pizza.jpg" http://localhost:8000/predict
```

## 2. AWS SageMaker (Enterprise)

python

```
# sagemaker_deploy.py
from sagemaker.pytorch import PyTorchModel

model = PyTorchModel(
    model_data="s3://bucket/foodvision.tar.gz",
    role="SageMakerRole",
    entry_point="inference.py",
    framework_version="2.0"
)
predictor = model.deploy(instance_type="ml.t3.medium")
```

## 3. Google Colab + ngrok (Quick Public API)

python

```
!pip install pyngrok
from pyngrok import ngrok
public_url = ngrok.connect(8000)
print(public_url)
```

# Mobile and Edge Deployment: Torch Mobile for Apps

## Export for Android/iOS

python

```
# Optimize for mobile
optimized_model =
torch.utils.mobile_optimizer.optimize_for_mobile(scripted_mode
l)
```

```
optimized_model._save_for_lite_interpreter("foodvision_mobile.
ptl")
```

### Android App (Kotlin)

kotlin
```
val module = Module.load(assetFilePath(context,
"foodvision_mobile.ptl"))
val inputTensor =
TensorImageUtils.bitmapToFloat32Tensor(bitmap, mean, std)
val outputTensor =
module.forward(IValue.from(inputTensor)).toTensor()
val scores = outputTensor.dataAsFloatArray
```

---

# Hands-On Milestone Project 3: Deploying FoodVision as a Live Web App

### Goal: FoodVision Pro — Live web app with:

- Camera upload
- Real-time prediction
- Confidence score
- Hosted on **Hugging Face Spaces**

---

### Final app.py

python
```
# app.py
import streamlit as st
import torch
import torchvision.transforms as T
from PIL import Image
```

```
import io
import numpy as np

# Load model
@st.cache_resource
def load_model():
    return torch.jit.load("foodvision_scripted.pt")

model = load_model()
model.eval()

# Transform
transform = T.Compose([
    T.Resize(256),
    T.CenterCrop(224),
    T.ToTensor(),
    T.Normalize(mean=[0.485, 0.456, 0.406], std=[0.229, 0.224,
0.225])
])

class_names = ['Pizza', 'Steak', 'Sushi']

st.set_page_config(page_title="FoodVision Pro",
page_icon="🍕")
st.title("🍔 FoodVision Pro")
st.write("Upload a food image or use your camera")

# Camera input
camera_image = st.camera_input("Take a photo")

# File upload
uploaded_file = st.file_uploader("Or upload an image",
type=["jpg", "jpeg", "png"])

img = None
if camera_image:
    img = Image.open(camera_image)
elif uploaded_file:
    img = Image.open(uploaded_file)
```

```python
if img:
    st.image(img, caption="Your Food", use_column_width=True)

    # Preprocess
    img_tensor = transform(img).unsqueeze(0)

    # Predict
    with torch.inference_mode():
        logits = model(img_tensor)
        probs = torch.softmax(logits, dim=1)
        pred_idx = probs.argmax(1).item()
        confidence = probs[0][pred_idx].item()

    st.markdown(f"### **Prediction: {class_names[pred_idx]}**")
    st.progress(confidence)
    st.write(f"**Confidence: {confidence:.1%}**")

    # Show all probabilities
    st.bar_chart({name: float(probs[0][i]) for i, name in
enumerate(class_names)})
```

---

## Deploy to Hugging Face Spaces

Create requirements.txt:

txt
```
torch
torchvision
streamlit
```

1. `pillow`

2. Push to GitHub
3. Create Space → **Streamlit** → Link repo

**Live URL**:
https://huggingface.co/spaces/yourname/foodvision-pro

# Security and Ethics: Bias Detection and Responsible AI Practices

## 1. Bias Check

python
```
# Check class distribution
from collections import Counter
labels = [label for _, label in test_dataset]
print(Counter(labels))
```

## 2. Fairness Metrics

python
```
from sklearn.metrics import confusion_matrix
cm = confusion_matrix(y_true, y_pred)
# Check if model confuses minority classes
```

## 3. Responsible AI Checklist

| Check | Done? |
|---|---|
| Data bias audited | Yes |
| Model card written | Yes |
| Privacy (no PII) | Yes |
| Fail-safe (low confidence → "I don't know") | Yes |

python
```
if confidence < 0.7:
   st.write("I'm not sure. Try another angle!")
```

## Common Mistakes to Avoid

| Mistake | Fix |
| --- | --- |
| **Deploying .pth directly** | Use TorchScript/ONNX |
| **Forgetting model.eval()** | Always in inference |
| **No input validation** | Check image size, type |
| **Hardcoded paths** | Use relative paths |
| **No error handling** | Wrap in try/except |
| **Ignoring mobile size** | Quantize + optimize |

## Real-World Applications

| App | Deployment |
| --- | --- |
| **Snapchat Filters** | Torch Mobile |
| **Google Lens** | ONNX + Cloud |
| **Doordash** | AWS SageMaker |
| **Tesla FSD** | Edge (custom chip) |

## Summary: Key Takeaways

1. **Export** with TorchScript, ONNX, quantization.
2. **Web** → Streamlit + Hugging Face Spaces.
3. **API** → FastAPI + ngrok.
4. **Cloud** → AWS, GCP.
5. **Mobile** → Torch Mobile + .ptl.
6. **Milestone 3**: FoodVision Pro live on HF Spaces.
7. **Ethics** → bias check, model card, confidence threshold.
8. **Production** = fast, small, secure, reliable.

---

## Practice Exercises

### Exercise 1: Deploy with FastAPI

Create /predict endpoint → test with curl.

### Exercise 2: Quantize Model

Compare size and speed:

python
```
import time
start = time.time()
pred = quantized_model(input)
print(f"Time: {time.time() - start:.4f}s")
```

### Exercise 3: Add "I Don't Know"

python
```
if confidence < 0.6:
    st.write("Unknown food. Try again!")
```

---

## Challenge: "FoodVision Mobile"

1. Export quantized .ptl model.
2. Build **Android app** with camera.
3. Run **on-device** (no internet).
4. Submit to **Google Play** (optional).

kotlin

```kotlin
// Use Android Studio + PyTorch Mobile
```

---

**Conclusion**: You are now a **full-stack deep learning engineer**.

You've gone from **zero to production AI**.

**Your Portfolio Now Includes**:

- 3 Milestone Projects
- GitHub + WandB + HF Spaces
- Live Web App
- Research Replication
- Production Code

**Next Step**: Apply to jobs.

You're ready.

---

**Your AI is live. The world is eating.**

# Conclusion

# Your Next Steps as a Deep Learning Engineer

You've built **neural networks from scratch**, trained **SOTA models**, tracked **100+ experiments**, replicated **research papers**, and deployed **production AI**.

Now, you're ready to **become a deep learning engineer**.

This chapter is your **career launchpad**:

- Build a **portfolio that gets interviews**.
- Ace **resumes**, **interviews**, and **salary negotiations**.
- Plan **continuous learning** in NLP, GANs, and RL.
- Access **resources** to stay ahead.

Let's turn your skills into a **high-paying job**.

---

## Building a Standout Portfolio: Showcasing Projects to Recruiters

Recruiters don't care about certificates.

They care about **what you've built**.

## The 3-Project Portfolio Formula

| Project | Why It Works |
|---|---|
| **FoodVision Mini** | CNN + transfer learning |
| **YOLO Food Detection** | Research replication |
| **FoodVision Pro (Live App)** | Full-stack deployment |

---

## Portfolio Structure (GitHub)

text

```
github.com/yourname/dl-portfolio/
├── foodvision-mini/          # CNN + transfer learning
├── yolo-food-detection/      # Paper replication
├── foodvision-pro/           # Streamlit + HF Spaces
├── README.md                 # 3-bullet intro
└── resume.pdf
```

### README.md Example

markdown

```
# Deep Learning Engineer Portfolio

- **FoodVision Pro**: Live web app classifying 100+ foods → [Live Demo](https://huggingface.co/spaces/yourname/foodvision-pro)
- **YOLO Food Detection**: Replicated YOLOv8 on custom data → mAP@50 = 0.91
- **Experiment Tracking**: 50+ runs with WandB → [Dashboard](https://wandb.ai/...)

**Tech**: PyTorch, EfficientNet, YOLOv8, Streamlit, AWS
```

---

## Add Live Demos

| Tool | Link |
|---|---|
| Hugging Face Spaces | huggingface.co/spaces/yourname/foodvision-pro |
| Gradio | gradio.live |
| Streamlit Cloud | share.streamlit.io |

**Recruiters test your app in 10 seconds**.
Make it **fast, beautiful, and working**.

---

## Add WandB Reports

markdown

```
## Experiment Dashboard
[View 50+ runs →](https://wandb.ai/yourname/foodvision-pizza-steak)
- Best model: EfficientNet-B0 (98.7% acc)
- Ablation: LR 0.001 > 0.0001
```

---

## Add a Blog Post

markdown

```
# How I Built a 98% Accurate Food Classifier with 300 Images
[Read on Medium →](https://medium.com/...)
```

---

# Job Hunt Strategies: Resumes, Interviews, and Salary Negotiation

## Resume: 1 Page, 3 Sections

```markdown
# John Doe – Deep Learning Engineer
john@doe.com | github.com/johndoe | linkedin.com/in/johndoe

## Projects
- **FoodVision Pro** – Live AI web app (PyTorch, Streamlit, HF Spaces) → 10k+ users
- **YOLO Food Detection** – Replicated CVPR paper, mAP@50 = 0.91
- **Experiment Tracking** – 50+ models compared via WandB

## Skills
PyTorch | EfficientNet | YOLOv8 | ONNX | AWS | Git | Docker

## Experience
ML Intern @ FoodTech Startup – Built image classifier (95% acc)
```

> **No fluff**. Only **projects with metrics**.

---

## Interview Prep: The 3 Question Types

| Type | Example | How to Answer |
|---|---|---|
| **Technical** | "Explain backpropagation" | Draw on whiteboard |
| **Project** | "Why did you choose EfficientNet?" | "Speed/accuracy trade-off" |

| **Beha vioral** | "Tell me about a failed experiment" | "Overfit → added dropout → 5% gain" |
|---|---|---|

## System Design Question

> **"Design a real-time food recognition system for a restaurant tablet"**

**Answer Structure**:

1. **Input**: Camera → 224x224 RGB
2. **Model**: EfficientNet-B0 (quantized)
3. **Backend**: FastAPI + ONNX
4. **Frontend**: Streamlit
5. **Scaling**: AWS Lambda + S3
6. **Monitoring**: Prometheus + Grafana

## Salary Negotiation

| Level | Base Salary | Total Comp |
|---|---|---|
| **Entry-Level** | $90k–$120k | $120k–$160k |
| **Mid-Level** | $130k–$180k | $180k–$250k |
| **Senior** | $180k–$250k | $300k–$400k+ |

> **Always ask**: "What's the full compensation package?"

# Continuous Learning: Advanced Topics in NLP, GANs, and Reinforcement Learning

You've mastered **vision**. Now expand.

## 1. NLP (Natural Language Processing)

| Project | Start With |
|---|---|
| Sentiment Analysis | transformers + BERT |
| Chatbot | Llama 2 + Gradio |
| Document QA | Haystack |

python
```
from transformers import pipeline
classifier = pipeline("sentiment-analysis")
classifier("I love this food!")  # → POSITIVE
```

---

## 2. GANs (Generative Adversarial Networks)

| Project | Paper |
|---|---|
| Face Generator | StyleGAN2 |
| Image-to-Image | Pix2Pix |
| DeepFake | First Order Model |

python
```
# Use PyTorch GAN Zoo
!git clone
https://github.com/facebookresearch/pytorch_GAN_zoo
```

---

## 3. Reinforcement Learning (RL)

| Project | Library |
|---|---|
| CartPole | Gym + Stable Baselines |
| Atari Games | RLlib |
| Robot Control | Isaac Gym |

python
```
import gym
env = gym.make("CartPole-v1")
```

---

## Learning Roadmap

| Month | Focus |
|---|---|
| 1–3 | NLP with Hugging Face |
| 4–6 | GANs + Diffusion Models |
| 7–9 | RL + Robotics |
| 10–12 | MLOps + K8s |

---

# Resources: PyTorch Docs, Communities, and Further Reading

## Official Docs

| Resource | Link |
|---|---|
| PyTorch | pytorch.org |
| TorchVision | pytorch.org/vision |
| PyTorch Lightning | lightning.ai |

---

## Communities

| Platform | Use |
|---|---|
| **Reddit** | r/MachineLearning, r/learnmachinelearning |
| **Discord** | PyTorch, Fast.ai |
| **Twitter** | Follow @pytorch, @huggingface |

---

## Courses & Books

| Resource | Type |
|---|---|
| Fast.ai | Free course |
| Deep Learning Specialization (Coursera) | Andrew Ng |

| *Deep Learning* by Goodfellow | Bible |
|---|---|

---

### Papers to Read

| Paper | Why |
|---|---|
| ResNet (2015) | Skip connections |
| YOLOv1 (2016) | Real-time detection |
| Transformers (2017) | NLP revolution |
| EfficientNet (2019) | Scaling laws |

---

## Common Mistakes to Avoid

| Mistake | Fix |
|---|---|
| **No live demo** | Deploy to HF Spaces |
| **Generic resume** | Add **metrics** |
| **No GitHub** | Push **all projects** |
| **Not negotiating** | Always counter-offer |
| **Stopping learning** | Do **1 project/month** |

---

## Summary: Key Takeaways

1. **Portfolio** = 3 deployed projects with **live demos**.
2. **Resume** = projects + metrics + GitHub link.
3. **Interviews** = explain **your code**, not theory.
4. **Salary** = negotiate total comp.
5. **Next**: NLP → GANs → RL.
6. **Resources** = PyTorch docs, Reddit, Fast.ai.
7. **You are ready — apply today**.

---

## Practice Exercises

### Exercise 1: Build Portfolio Website

Use **GitHub Pages**:

markdown
```
# My DL Portfolio
[FoodVision Pro →](https://huggingface.co/spaces/...)
```

### Exercise 2: Mock Interview

Record yourself answering:

> "Explain how you built FoodVision Pro end-to-end."

### Exercise 3: Apply to 5 Jobs

Use:

- LinkedIn
- Indeed
- Wellfound (AngelList)

---

## Challenge: “The 30-Day Job Sprint”

| Day | Task |
| --- | --- |
| 1–5 | Polish 3 projects |
| 6–10 | Write resume + LinkedIn |
| 11–15 | Apply to 20 jobs |
| 16–20 | Practice 5 mock interviews |
| 21–25 | Build 1 new project (e.g., chatbot) |
| 26–30 | Follow up + negotiate offers |

**Goal**: **1 job offer in 30 days**.

---

**You did it.**

You went from **zero to production AI**.

Now go get that **$150k+ job**.

**The future of AI needs you.**

---

**Final Words**:

“The best way to predict the future is to invent it.”

— Alan Kay

**You just did.**

Now **ship it**.

www.ingramcontent.com/pod-product-compliance
Lightning Source LLC
LaVergne TN
LVHW060037210926
848481LV00013B/3889